SCANDAL

How homosexuality became a crime

David Boyle

THE REAL PRESS
www.therealpress.com

Published as print on demand and in various ebook formats in Great Britain in 2016 by the Real Press.

ISBN: 978-0955226373 (print)

Cover design by Hodge Creative Ltd.

In memory of my Irish forebears

1

It was Saturday 6 April 1895. The weather was windy and drizzly as the passengers packed onto the quayside at Dover to catch the steam packet to Calais, due on the evening tide. Perhaps it was packed that night because of Easter the following week. Perhaps it wasn't as packed as some of the witnesses claimed later, or the downright gossips who weren't actually there. But it was still full. Those waiting on the quay wrapped up warm against the chilly Channel breeze and eyed each other nervously, afraid to meet anyone they knew, desperately wanting to remain anonymous.

Among those heading for France that night was an American, Henry Harland, the editor and co-founder of the notorious quarterly known as *The Yellow Book*, the journal of avant garde art and writing which had taken England by the scruff of the neck in the 1890s. Harland had come to Europe with his wife Aline, pretending to have been born in St Petersburg and planning to live in Paris, but had instead made his London flat, at 144 Cromwell Road, the very hive of excitement in the literary world. Henry James, Edmund Gosse and Aubrey Beardsley came and went. The parties were talked about with awe and excitement. Henry and Aline always spent the spring in Paris, so they were not leaving the country suddenly and in desperation, but it dawned on them that the reason the quayside was so packed that night was because many others were.

The name of the ferry the Harlands boarded has been lost to history. It was probably the *Victoria* – her sister ship the *Empress* had been badly damaged in a collision the month before and was now in dry dock. There she heaved beside the sea wall, as the muffled passengers filed up the gangway, her twin rakish masts and her twin funnels belching smoke, her two paddlewheels poised to drive across the world's busiest sea lane at 18 knots, her stern flag flapping in the wind with the insignia of the London, Chatham and Dover Railway.

Harland had a good idea why the ferries were full, though he was still surprised. He was also aware of at least some of the implications for himself. Oscar Wilde had been arrested for 'gross indecency' that evening, having lost his libel action the day before. The news of the warrant for his arrest was in the evening papers, and included the information that Wilde had been arrested while he had been reading a copy of *The Yellow Book* (this was quite wrong, in fact; he was reading *Aphrodite* by Pierre Louys). Harland could only guess the motivations of those who were now suddenly crowding across the English Channel, but it looked remarkably like fear. They huddled in corners in the stateroom downstairs, out of the wind, damp and smuts, wondering perhaps whether they would ever see their native land again.

There was an unnerving atmosphere of menace that evening. One item in the evening papers implied that the nation was perched on the edge of a scandal that would make the establishment teeter. "If the rumours which are abroad tonight are proved to be correct we shall have such an exposure as has been unheard of in this country for many years past."

Did it mean the exposure would reach those who run the nation, or did it mean something even more terrifying – that the exposure would spread downwards through society? As the passengers knew only too well, the combination of events which they had feared for a decade had now come to pass. It had been a few months short of ten years since the so-called 'Labouchère amendment' had been rushed through the House of Commons, criminalising homosexual activity of any kind between men. It was never quite clear why women were excluded – there is no evidence for the old story that Queen Victoria claimed it was impossible. For ten years now, they had watched the rising sense of outrage at the very idea of 'homosexuality' – though the term was not yet in common use – and had realised that there might come a time when that law was enforced with an unsurpassed ferocity.

It wasn't that they necessarily had anything to be ashamed of – quite the reverse – but they had reputations to be lived down, some event in their past or some 'unfortunate' relationship behind them. Now that public concern had turned to what looked like public hysteria, they clearly had to be vigilant. They did not want to be accused, as Oscar Wilde was accused, by a violent aristocrat of doubtful sanity, and would then have to respond in the courts or the press. They could not face the fatal knock on the front door from a smiling acquaintance who would turn out to be a dangerous blackmailer.

But now the unthinkable had happened. Wilde had been stupid enough to sue the Marquess of Queensberry for libel, and had lost. The public had driven each other into a crescendo of rage and it seemed only sensible to lie low in Paris for a while. Or Nice or Dieppe, or the place where the British tended to go in flight from the law – Madrid. Anywhere they could be beyond the reach of the British legal system.

As we shall see, one of those who fled, as I discovered during the research that led to this book, was my own great-great-grandfather – escaping for the second time in a just over a decade, in a story that my own family had suppressed for three generations.

*

It is no small matter to flee your home and go abroad, especially to do so within the space of a few hours to gather your belongings and make arrangements for your property or your money. As it is, escape was only a solution available to those wealthy enough to flee. It is even tougher perhaps for those in some kind of unconventional relationship, ambiguous to the outside world – but perhaps not ambiguous enough – aware that the decision to go was probably irreversible. It might look like an admission of guilt.

On the other hand, what might happen when the newspapers could unleash this kind of bile? What would happen when they had successfully gaoled Wilde with hard labour and turned on his friends, and anyone else who looked unusual? What would happen if the rumours were correct and the scandal would shortly engulf the government and royal family? Harland did not know at this stage that, when the news about *The Yellow Book* became clear on Monday morning, a mob would gather outside the offices of his publishers Bodley Head, and would break all the windows. "It killed *The Yellow Book* and it nearly killed me," said publisher John Lane later.

We know now that, in the event, the threatened conflagration did not take place, but in the remaining 72 years while Section 11 of the Criminal Law Amendment Act, the Labouchère Amendment, stayed on the statute books, 75,000 were prosecuted under its terms, among them John Gielgud, Lord Montagu and Alan Turing. Many thousands of lives were ruined – Turing committed suicide not long afterwards, having been forced to undergo hormone treatment that made him grow breasts.

Yet that moment of fear in Britain in 1895, unprecedented in modern times, has been largely forgotten. It is remembered as a sniggering remnant of gossip, about the number of English aristocrats or others in public life, living incognito in Dieppe, or glimpsed in the bars in Paris, and the awareness as a result that they had something to hide. One of the purposes of this book is to remember it for what it was – one of the most disturbing chapters in modern English history, when public horror at sexual behaviour reached such intensity that nobody seemed completely safe, and nobody could be relied on to protect you. And when a man like Wilde, the darling of the theatre critics, with two sell-out shows in London's West End theatres, could be brought low by a furious, litigious pugilist – well, really, who was safe?

This unique moment of fear in English history came at a peculiar moment, at perhaps the apogee of tolerance in so many other ways – women were cycling and getting university degrees, training to be doctors. Mohandas Gandhi was a London-trained barrister working in South Africa. George Bernard Shaw was overturning assumptions about the right way to dress, eat and spell. H. G. Wells was sleeping his way through the ranks of the young female Fabians. Edward Carpenter, in his sandals, was advertising freedom from the constraints of conventional sexuality, having forged a gay relationship with a working class man from Sheffield. William Morris was still, just, preaching a revolution based on medieval arts and crafts. And yet the rage at the idea that men should love each other sexually threatened to overwhelm everything.

That morning, Queensberry had received a telegram from an anonymous supporter, which read: "Every man in the City is with you. Kill the bugger."

Why did it happen? Partly because of growing public concern following the Labouchère amendment, sneaked though Parliament in 1885, but even that was more than the individual brainchild of a lone radical. Why this shift from tolerance of the changing role of women and emerging new ideas to this threatening public rage? How did homosexuality emerge as a key issue in English public life?

The answer lies in the events that took place in Dublin a decade before, starting with the political aftermath of the murder of Lord Frederick Cavendish, the son of the Duke of Devonshire and the newly-appointed Chief Secretary to Ireland.

*

But I had a more personal reason for finding out the answers to some of these questions. My family lived in Dublin in the 1880s. The reason that they don't any more, and that I was born in England not Ireland, was because of those same events there in that decade. Until the last few years, when I began researching this book, I was unaware of them.

All I knew was that my great-great-grandfather, the banker Richard Boyle, had left Dublin suddenly and under a cloud around 1884. His photograph has been torn out of the family photo album, with only his forehead remaining. There are no likenesses of him anywhere that I know about. The letters related to these events in the family, and what followed, have long since been destroyed. I believe I was even there when my grandfather burned the last of them on the bonfire around 1975.

I had always been interested in what might have happened, but had assumed that the memories were now beyond recovery, just as the fate of my great-great-grandfather was lost in the mists of unfathomable time.

As it turned out, I was wrong. I was working on another incident in Irish history in the British Library, and discovered as I did so that a whole raft of Victorian Irish newspapers had been digitised and were now searchable online. On an impulse, I put in the name 'Richard Boyle' and searched through the references in the Dublin papers. Then, suddenly, my heart began beating a little faster, because there it was – the first clue I found to a personal tragedy, and a national tragedy too: this was the spark that lit the fuse which led to the criminalisation of gay behaviour and the great moment of fear that followed the arrest of Oscar Wilde. That first clue led to others, which led to others. I will never know the whole story, but what I did discover took me on a historical rollercoaster, and an emotional one, which catapulted me back to the strangely familiar world of the end of the nineteenth century – and a glimpse of that sudden fear in April 1895 that drove many of those affected so suddenly abroad.

2

*"How could any Irish gentleman be free from horrible charges
when a man of this character is in Dublin, rifling about to
right and left."*

**Sir George Trevelyan, Chief Secretary for Ireland, describing the
activities of John Meiklejohn, April 1884.**

The peculiar series of events that led to the criminalisation of
homosexual acts in 1885 began with a terrorist act in Phoenix
Park three years before. Lord Frederick Cavendish had only
been in Ireland as Chief Secretary for a matter of hours before
he set out for a walk with Thomas Henry Burke, the under-
secretary to the Lord Lieutenant. Burke was on the death list of
a new Irish nationalist organisation calling themselves the
Invincibles. Burke was pointed out by a Dublin town
councillor called James Carey (who later turned Queen's
evidence against his colleagues) and the nine-strong team of
assassins attacked him with knives. They did not recognise
Cavendish, but he was killed because he was there.

The Phoenix Park murders, as they were called, were the
latest twist in the tortured succession of Irish politics. It was
culmination of growing tension that followed the activities of
the extra-parliamentary Land League, the widespread rent

strike, the intolerance of the Coercion Act, and the resulting imprisonment of the Irish nationalist leader Charles Stewart Parnell and all the League's leaders in Kilmainham Gaol in 1881.

The murders changed everything. It put the constitutional nationalists seriously on the back foot. "How can I carry on a public agitation if I am stabbed in the back in this way?" asked Parnell.

Dublin was by then a city of intrigue and secrecy, bitterly divided politically. But even in Westminster, there was a new radical spirit abroad. The year after the murders, the great radical Joseph Chamberlain uttered the explosive description of the Conservative leader Lord Salisbury: "The spokesman of a class – a class to which he himself belongs, *who toil not neither do they spin.*" It was a declaration of war against the landowning classes and the Dublin elite were, above all, landowners. It was the explosive driving force of division in Ireland. Richard Boyle was a landowner as well as a banker. He owned more than 235 acres in County Waterford.

Parnell – the 'Uncrowned King of Ireland' – led 62 MPs in occasional alliance with Gladstone's Liberals. Gladstone was contemplating the idea of Home Rule for Ireland that would split his own party just a few years later. Parnell was already engaged in his affair with Kitty O'Shea, which would bring about his own downfall and torpedo a solution to the running sore of Irish politics. For the first time in British parliamentary politics, sex scandal was about to determine events, and it was the same in Dublin.

But the real undercurrent of violence and peril that lay just below the surface in Ireland was only too obvious in the city too. Dublin included the worst poverty in Europe – a third of the city was living in squalor – but it was a fearful city too. What might home rule, or Chamberlain's National Council for Ireland, mean in practice for the Unionist land-owning class? What would happen to a nation where the city population could cheer the Mad Mahdi, the Muslim extremist of the day, during the royal visit in 1885? What would majority rule mean for their privileged and safe existence, secured in extremis by the bayonets of the Royal Irish Fusiliers?

History suggests that Gladstone's home rule failure was a giant tragedy, but at the time it looked more like potential civil war averted. Those in charge in Dublin would not have known the future, but they feared their society was in its final decades – and of course it was.

Partly because of these tensions, Dublin was just emerging as a city of culture. Not just the drawing room renditions of 'Poor Wandering One', but in writing and the arts. Oscar Wilde was conducting his courtship of Constance Lloyd in Dublin during the months of this story. She was visiting Dublin in the early part of 1884, when Wilde was lecturing at the Gaiety Theatre. Also in the audience was the eighteen-year-old poet W. B. Yeats.

But among the secrets of the city was the gay scene. 'Homosexuality' was not a word in common use. Nor was it a concept that was widely understood: the charge which the Nationalists flung at the Unionists now, and for decades after these events, was about indecent *acts* – it was about behaviour, not about different ways of being. The French critic Michel Foucault has argued that 'homosexuality' was an early twentieth century invention and the debate in Dublin bears this out. It is what people did that worried their contemporaries, not what people were.

Either way, the behaviour was unlikely to have been more prevalent in Dublin than anywhere else. Men met men, after all, as they always had. But because of what was about to take place, we know a little more about it. At one end of the scale there were the homosexual brothels, near the barracks, and the public toilets which had become places for picking up young men. Judging by the evidence at the trials that marked the culmination of these events, there were also the possibilities emerging from walks in the Botanic Gardens on a Sunday afternoon. But most gay encounters took place among the upper middle classes as an adjunct to dinner parties, a little groping in the cab going home afterwards, or after long walks home through the suburbs to lodgings in town.

Mild stuff, but – as it turned out – potentially explosive. The trouble was, for those who worried about such things, that gay behaviour was not actually against the law. The only area which the law condemned was sodomy, which had been punishable by death, if you could prove it, since the days of Henry VIII – until 1861, when the death sentence was abolished for this and a raft of other offences. But proof was extremely difficult in cases like this. In fact, it was the problems the prosecutors faced in Dublin – demonstrating beyond reasonable doubt that something very specific and physical, and necessarily private, had happened – that led to the 1885 change in the law, as we shall see.

*

So the scene is now set for our tragedy. Political oppositions have a habit of flinging sexual allegations at those in power. There are some allegations, even today, which are so unpleasant that just to accuse someone of them almost dispenses with the need for proof. Every generation has crimes like this. In our day, this is sometimes the case if the allegations involve child abuse. There are places when accusing those in power of homosexuality can drag them down from authority. It is a potent political weapon, but a double-edged one. By invoking the mob, it can also lead to a terrifying rise in tension among innocent people, or among unconventional people who love each other in different ways.

Ireland in 1884 was one of the early examples of this in modern times, and it was a political reaction to the assassination of Cavendish and Burke. The horror of the killing, in cold blood in the heart of respectable Dublin, had forced the Nationalists, the constitutional republicans, onto the defensive. There was a conscious search somehow for a way of clawing back the moral high ground. The self-appointed agent of this objective was the new Nationalist MP for Mallon, William O'Brien, a serial founder of propaganda newspapers and a journalist whose particular style can be deduced from his nickname, 'Screaming William'.

O'Brien's weekly newspaper *United Ireland* was mainly a vituperative commentary on the evils of the British-dominated Irish Civil Service. In August 1883, his unsigned editorial identified their new campaign, an attack on the homosexual proclivities of James Ellis French, the director of the detective branch of the Royal Irish Constabulary, the man in charge of the Phoenix Park investigation. The editorial was actually written by the Nationalist MP Timothy Healy, a future governor-general of the Irish state.

French came from Cork, like O'Brien, and his reputation in the RIC was such that new cadets were often warned about him when they started there. The editorial compared him with an Irish civil servant called Corry Connellan, who had fled the country after being accused of homosexuality sixteen years before.

The Unionists were horrified and urged French to sue which, very reluctantly, he did. But he was in a deeply nervous state, and in the midst of what we would now call a nervous breakdown, and he delayed for so long that the case was dismissed. He was also declared medically unfit and dismissed from his job.

The Unionist establishment wanted a libel action to put O'Brien in his place, but O'Brien wanted to be sued as well and had been preparing his ground for court by employing a former Scotland Yard detective, former Chief Inspector John Meiklejohn – O'Brien's fearsome memoirs *Evening Memories* call him Micklejohn. Meiklejohn was not an ordinary detective. He had been dismissed and imprisoned for two years hard labour for bribery. He was embittered and badly in need of money. In 1877, he had been arrested for accepting bribes from two confidence tricksters to keep them informed about investigations into their activities. He also had an unsavoury reputation for blackmail.

Through the winter of 1883/4, Meiklejohn criss-crossed between London and Dublin, and his balding head and twirling moustaches became a familiar sight in the bars along the Liffey. His investigations took him to the heart of the cosy world of the Dublin upper middle classes. His methods were tough, and he was supported by O'Brien's energetic solicitors. Here was a tragedy in the making.

O'Brien also had a fanatical horror of homosexuality and he was determined not to let the issue drop. Armed with information from Meiklejohn, he opened up another front. Another unsigned editorial on 10 May 1884 singled out the Secretary of the General Post Office in Dublin, Gustavus Cornwall. He quoted a remark which Cornwall had allegedly made to his friends, after crossing Meiklejohn's investigation: "This is no longer a country in which a gentleman may live".

The article was full of innuendo. O'Brien referred to "an official of his tastes". He also described an unnamed military officer who would "find it hard to bear the pangs of separation" if Cornwall skipped the country. At the end of the article, O'Brien challenged him to sue. "There is a chance for you, Mr CORNWALL."

Cornwall kept his head down. So O'Brien took his campaign to Westminster, naming him in a series of interventions in the House of Commons, protected by Parliamentary privilege. Something had to be done and Cornwall was prevailed upon by his friends to act. "Before we have finished we shall turn every nook and close of Dublin Castle inside out until the world shall shriek with horror," wrote an exultant O'Brien. Dublin Castle here stands for the whole elite that ran the Irish administration in the city.

Cornwall's closest friends were already nervous. He had many friends, and was well-known as a brilliant host and entertainer, witty and urbane, with a particular penchant for music. He was a lynchpin. He had to win the case.

O'Brien used the six weeks before the case came to trial to raise the rhetoric, despite fines for contempt of court. On 7 June, he increased the temperature considerably, describing a "system of depravity unsurpassed in the history of human crime". He contrasted Cornwall's supposed activities with the lesser crimes of the Moonlighters and Invincibles, those responsible for the Phoenix Park murders and similar outrages.

This was extreme stuff. According to O'Brien, homosexual behaviour among the governing classes was *worse* than politically motivated murder. But he said the same in the House of Commons a week later and the Nationalist MPs around him shouted "hear, hear!"

The Dublin elite were nervous, for obvious reasons. They were not just frightened of being exposed personally. Their fear was that people would be unfairly caught up in the whole scandal because of the brutish and intrusive investigation by Meiklejohn and his team. "How could any Irish gentleman be free from horrible charges when a man of this character was in Dublin, rifling about to right and left," said the Chief Secretary for Ireland, Sir George Trevelyan. These were worrying times.

*

The case opened on 2 July with enormous press attention. Meiklejohn and O'Brien's defence team had bullied three key witnesses into appearing, despite the inevitable damage to their lives and careers. There was a twenty-one year-old called Malcolm Johnston, also known in gay circles as 'Conny' or the 'Maid of Athens'. There was also George Taylor, 33, who worked for the B&I shipping line. There was also Alfred McKiernan, a clerk at Munster Bank (the spellings are various so I am sticking to these).

Munster Bank had two branches in Dublin, and one of them shared the premises at 35 College Green with Richard Boyle's family bank, Boyle, Low, Murray & Co. Both Munster branches were managed by another colourful character, a regular visitor to 35 College Green and a well-known speculator in the Dublin Stock Exchange. This was Robert Farquharson, a bachelor and another inveterate thrower of dinner parties at his home at Dromana, 57 Leeson Park – a key figure in the Unionist musical dinner party circuit.

McKiernan was important here. It isn't clear which of the two Munster Bank branches he worked at, but he had worked there for more than a decade and was part of the dinner party circuit too. He had what was described as "a beautiful voice" and often sang after dinner. He lived in Pembroke Road and had met Cornwall at a 'musical' dinner party in Raglan Road eight years before, when his wife was away. Malcolm Johnston had met Cornwall on Whit Monday 1881, and had ended up inevitably at the Botanic Gardens, and it was in the hansom cab home that some of the disputed events took place.

The three witnesses briefly refused to go into the witness box, and were threatened by O'Brien's solicitors. Then it was Taylor's evidence that seemed to become symbolic of the whole case, describing in detail another visit to the Dublin's Botanic Gardens on Boxing Day 1881 with Cornwall and Martin Kirwan, a well-connected and aristocratic officer in the Royal Dublin Fusiliers. Taylor explained that, in their circles, Kirwan was known as 'Lizzie' and Cornwall was known as 'The Duchess'. This particular visit involved a trip inside the hothouse; afterwards, under a holly tree, Cornwall was supposed to have taken "improper liberties".

But Cornwall was extraordinarily controlled and self-possessed in the face of this and other evidence, despite gushing letters to McKiernan. He was also accused picking up a man at the urinal in College Green, just opposite Boyle, Low, Murray & Co.

"I have never been in that urinal in my life," said Cornwall.

"It is alleged," said Cornwall's barrister, "that in December '81, at three o'clock in the afternoon, in the Botanic

Gardens, you solicited a person to commit the same offence (buggery) and indecently touched his person. Is there a particle of truth in that?"

"Absolutely none. It is false," said Cornwall. Even O'Brien was impressed with his coolness, but it wasn't enough. After five days of evidence, the jury took just an hour to decide for O'Brien. What happened next explains to some extent the ensuing panic in the Unionist community, and especially among anyone connected with the people involved or named in the trial. The moment the verdict was announced, there was tumultuous cheering in the crowds waiting in the courtyard. O'Brien took a coach to the Imperial Hotel in Sackville Street, where he was staying, past cheering crowds lining the bridges and streets, and people waving from every window. A band greeted him outside the hotel. In towns all over Ireland, crowds began to gather. Reports of bands playing in celebration came from Boyle, Charleville, Cork, Dungarven, Edenderry, Limerick, Longford and Newcastle West. There were tar barrels lit in the streets of Armagh and Cork and bonfires in other places. Money began to pour into the offices of *United Ireland* to cover O'Brien's costs. Organisations great and small, and especially Roman Catholic or working men's ones, passed motions of fervent congratulation. One of them urged congratulations on O'Brien for "his struggle to the death to expose the vile perpetrators of the loathsome, impure, and revolting crimes which belong almost exclusively to the official classes".

That was important. For 'official classes' we have to read the languid ascendancy.

O'Brien spelled out the political message in his newspaper:

"May we not cherish the dream, that the same force of honest Irish indignation which has lashed the wretched CORNWALL and his leprous associates from the island as with whips of scorpions, will yet rise up ... and sweep into the sea the whole fabric of English rule within which the dark brood of CORNWALLS and FRENCHES have had their birth and nurture?"

The *Kerry Independent* called Cornwall "one of the lowest scums of the earth". The *Dublin Evening Telegraph* criticised French's detective department for not investigating and letting Cornwall bear the whole "odium of contaminating the running stream of Irish moral purity by stirring up the sink of pollution implanted by foreign hands at its very edges".

Even the Unionist *Dublin Daily Express* described how Cornwall "must sink to the lowest depth of detestable depravity in the estimation of every man of moral instincts and the sense of virtue which is natural in civilised community, to say nothing of religious convictions."

This unprecedented public hysteria, and the threat of mob rage, must have utterly terrified anyone with any connection to the people involved in the case, whether or not they had actually been connected into Cornwall's close-knit gay friendships. It was an extraordinary prefiguration of the scenes of hysteria after Oscar Wilde's trial a decade later, which followed a similar abortive libel action. Wilde himself was in London by July 1884, but he seems to have taken note.

Cornwall meanwhile fled to Scotland to stay with his brother-in-law, Sir Robert Dalyell, and the pressure mounted on the government to do something. Parnell himself raised it in Parliament. Was Cornwall going to be prosecuted? What about his friends?

*

On Saturday 12 July, the government finally acted. The Irish police swooped on Cornwall in Scotland and arrested him, just before supper on Sunday night. On Monday morning, he was back in Dublin, arriving at Kingstown docks by mail boat, and taken by train and then taxi to Store Street police station. French was arrested outside Cork the following day. McKiernan, the cashier and witness who had ensured their downfall, was sacked by Munster Bank.

Back in Dublin, James Ellis French arrived from Cork on Wednesday, also now under arrest. Three young men, two of them unemployed, were interrogated by detectives and warned not to leave. Martin Kirwan was arrested, along with an army surgeon – a major in the Grenadier Guards – called Albert de Fernandez, who was arrested by detectives in London at Chelsea Barracks. In those days, it took only a matter of a few weeks to come to trial, and so it was that – three weeks after the first recorded tennis tournament in history, and three days after the foundation stone was laid for the Statue of Liberty – eight men went on trial in the Green Street Court House in Dublin. Three of them were accused of running homosexual brothels, one in Ship Street, one at 43 Golden Lane, both near Ship Street Barracks, and one at 56 Lower Rathmines Road.

*

It was 8 August and a warm summer's day. The Irish polo tournament, a key moment in the Dublin social calendar, was being played at Phoenix Park. One defendant, the 70-year-old Quaker wine merchant and grocer James Pillar, was charged with eight different counts of conspiracy and felony. "A more horrible description I never yet read of the acts of any human being in the whole of my lengthened experience," said the judge, Mr Baron Dowse (Baron was his first name, not his title).

Pillar made what turned out to be the huge mistake of pleading guilty. He stood in the dock, white-lipped and trembling, as well he might have done having heard the mob outside. Next to him, James Ellis French was dishevelled and drooling a little, part of what Parnell claimed was a sophisticated act to prove himself unfit to stand trial on the grounds of "softening of the brain".

Exactly what was said during the trail is hard to discover because the judge asked the newspapers not to report the salacious evidence and the court records were burned in 1922, along with the rest of Ireland's public records – the act of a departing British administration. But the innuendo was reported: the musical activities of the defendants were wielded to great effect. The prosecuting counsel remarked to Kirwan under cross-examination, that "you are all musical". The word took on an added weight of meaning in that sentence, and the same innuendo was taken up later by the Nationalist MPs.

The case was also extremely confused, especially given how difficult it was to prove something very specific like sodomy. Cornwall's legal team brought evidence from three doctors to show that, as described, this was physically impossible in the confines of a hansom cab. He and Kirwan were later acquitted of conspiracy as well, when their barristers demonstrated that the three witnesses had been threatened by O'Brien's solicitors. The blind former schoolteacher Daniel Considine and the ragged, elderly Robert Fowler, were both found guilty of 'keeping a disorderly house' and sentenced to two years hard labour.

Pillar, who had pleaded guilty to sodomy, was sentenced to twenty years penal servitude. I have been unable to find out how long he survived this ordeal, which was effectively a death sentence.

Jurors and medical experts alike could not agree whether French was sane enough to stand trial. It was not until the end of his third trial on 20 December that he was finally found guilty and sentenced to two years hard labour.

Cornwall left immediately for England and, from that safer haven, attempted to rescue his reputation by demanding that his libel case be re-opened. The judge replied that, although he had been acquitted of sodomy, he was clearly guilty of "vices and practices equally loathsome that should cause him to be shunned by all persons having regard to decency."

The judge went on, describing a situation where "a vile gang existed in the city, leagued together for the pursuit of unnatural depravity and vice, and that Cornwall was one of that gang". In fact, most of Cornwall's friends in the 'vile gang' – and we must assume Richard Boyle's friends too – had been acquitted. But the damage had been done. Beyond that, reconstructing more than those basic facts, from the delicacies of the reporting by the Dublin press, proved extremely hard.

I could also see very little, at that stage, about how the story would have impacted on my own forebears. I assumed I would never know.

3

"It is announced this week that Mr Boyle has made his home beyond the Pyrenees."
The Nation, 23 August 1884

I had never heard of the so-called 'Dublin Scandals' before I walked into the British Library to do my research on something entirely different. It was a whim that made me put my great-grand-father's name into the search engine for the Dublin newspapers for the 1880s, having always wondered what became of him. And as I searched through the references, the following suddenly came up in the *Nation* for 23 August 1884:

"Mr Richard W. Boyle, the Dublin banker whose name is associated with the scandals at present under investigation in Green-street, is a gentleman who prefers a 'castle in Spain' to a residence in the Irish metropolis. It is announced this week that Mr Boyle has made his home beyond the Pyrenees."

I think I took a deep breath. It was exciting to finally have a clue to his sudden departure from Ireland, but in itself the snippet was pretty obscure. "The scandals at present under investigation in Green-street," told me next to nothing. But the date was useful. The word 'scandal' in Dublin that August, as it turned out, could mean only one scandal. It was frustrating to know relatively little because of the reporting restrictions, but also because – perhaps because it happened in Ireland – the Dublin Scandals, or 'Dublin Castle Scandals', have largely been forgotten in England. I read the very few accounts written by modern historians. I read the reports in the Dublin newspapers, and the hysterical editorials in *United Ireland*, and that seemed to be that.

But again, I was wrong. What happened was that the trials had carried on throughout August and – in the case of James Ellis French – for the rest of the year. And once the stuff about whether sodomy was possible in a cab was over, the press had relaxed a little. And, in particular, the newspapers in what is now Northern Ireland seemed to be less reluctant to report. And so it was that my own family's involvement began to be clearer, thanks to a series of reports in *Freeman's Journal* and the *Dublin Evening Post*.

*

Before I set out what those reports revealed, let me say something about my own family, and my great-great-grandfather in particular. My part of the Boyle family was not originally Irish, but Scottish. They emigrated to the north of Ireland during the seventeenth century, part of the Plantation of Ulster with protestant families under James I. The family, which settled in and around the small town of Limavady in County Londonderry, appears to be descended from the lairds of Kelburn – the family from where the earls of Glasgow eventually sprung – and for several generations were tanners, among them the James Boyle who was elected provost of Limavady four times between 1660 and his death in 1719.

With the march of time, the family fortunes improved and James Boyle's great-grandson, the first to be called Alexander, helped materially by a runaway marriage with the eighteen-year-old heiress Grace Vicars. Here the banking future of his son and grandson were decided when Grace's sister, Elizabeth, married Peter La Touche of the La Touche Bank (forerunner of the Bank of Ireland), a generous man who was more than pleased to help his nephews. And so it was that by the Victorian age Alexander's son, always know as Alex Boyle the Banker, was living in St Stephen's Green at the heart of Dublin.

These were Protestants in a Catholic nation, of course, sometimes living as country gentlemen in big draughty houses, sometimes in more modest homes, ministered to by an alien Church of Ireland, supported unwillingly by tithes on the indigenous population. It was a land of horses and fairies, Resident Magistrates and superstition, emerald green hills and forced evictions. The Great Irish Potato Famine was still within living memory during the events described below.

Alex Boyle is the other side of the horizon of memory, but we can work out a little about him from the fact that he was accorded the rare privilege of becoming a life member of the Royal Dublin Society at the age of only 24 (Peter La Touche was one of his sponsors). The RDS was, and is, the equivalent of the Royal Society of Arts in London, and its forerunner. Its purpose is to encourage practical, intellectual ferment. Alex Boyle was not just respected; he was something of an innovator and investor, and among the people he supported financially was the Irish inventor, Sir James Caleb Anderson.

By profession, he was a banker, and a partner in the firm of Boyle, Low, Pim and Co., since 1840 based at 35 College Green, Dublin. He was also a governor of the Royal Hospital for Incurables at Donnybrook and was for a time Dublin City Sheriff. By the 1860s, Alexander and his wife Helen were living with their five children – Alexander, Richard, Edward, Margaret and Mary – at 13 Upper Merrion Street. The partnership had morphed into Boyle, Low, Murray and Co. and was more a banking agency than a bank, specialising in financing new ventures and in stockbroking, and his second son was being groomed to succeed him (for some reason Alexander, the eldest, didn't – he ran an oyster fishing business). In the last years of his life, Alex Boyle lived at 12 Earlsfort Terrace, with a country house at Eathine, Bray.

He died on 14 January 1870. His granddaughter said later that he was a kindly and generous man, much mourned by the many family friends and well-known Dublin people whom he had helped financially. We have to take this kind of Victorian rhetoric with a bit of a pinch of salt, but he often failed to ask for repayment, judging by the number of IOUs found in a case after his death. His obituary talked about his conversational charm, but described him also "a strict disciplinarian and a great economist of time".

Which brings us on to Richard Warneford Boyle, known to the family as 'Dick', brought into the world and moulded by a man who was very economical with his time. Among the many things we don't know about him was what he looked like, though we can guess – perhaps tall and slightly cadaverous like the rest of my family. But we do know some things. He was born in 1837, the year that Queen Victoria came to the throne, the very dawn of the Victorian age. He married at the respectable age of 31 to Alice Chambers, whose wealthy family came from Clough House in Rotherham in Yorkshire.

We know he was a dutiful son. He followed his father as chairman of the Dublin Stock Exchange. He called his eldest son after his father and his eldest daughter, his first child Helen – born at Earlsfort Terrace in 1869 – after his mother. It is extraordinary, as I discovered later, how much the family was wedded to the bank. 'Alexander Boyle the Younger', Richard's father, was co-signatory to his son's marriage contract along with his partner, James Marshall Murray. James' successor John Marshall Murray carried on paying Richard's life insurance premiums after his disappearance as a way of supporting Alice. This truly was a marriage underwritten by the bank.

But three other things emerge about Richard Warneford Boyle out of this picture of Victorian respectability.

First, he was fascinated by health. He was not just on the board of the South Dublin Union – the workhouse – but on the managing committee of the National Orthopaedic Hospital and the Cork Street Fever Hospital, raising money for more facilities to tackle a smallpox outbreak and other things besides. He worked with the Royal College of Surgeons in Ireland to found an annual award. Like his father, and his daughter Helen after him, he was a progressive thinker. He wanted to make things happen in this strange divided city.

Second, he was an ambitious Unionist. He represented the south of Dublin on the town council. He was a popular and vigorous member of the Unionist elite which ran Dublin. We glimpse him seconding a motion to open the museums and galleries of the city on Sundays, or acting as treasurer for a banquet in honour of General Sir Garnet Wolesley, who was about to depart as this story begins for the Nile Campaign to rescue General Gordon. Ironically, one of his fellow organisers for this was the future judge at the trial at the heart of this story, Baron Dowse.

Third, he had at least a charismatic edge. We see him proposing motions and votes of thanks, for the 'manly' way in which the Lord Mayor had defended the city – referring probably to the Phoenix Park murders – for introducing Unionist speakers and proposing Conservative candidates, making blood-thirsty noises about the dangers of the Nationalist leader Charles Stewart Parnell. But he was not an unthinking Conservative: he was one of 60 signatories, mainly protestants, who signed the first resolution, on 19 May 1870, calling for home rule for Ireland on the grounds that "the attempt to assert consolidation on the Irish people, to destroy their individuality, has been simply disastrous ... we want connection with England, but we will no longer have our domestic affairs committed to a London parliament".

This is only the first elusive paradox in this story. He was a Conservative Unionist councillor in Dublin who also helped launch the Home Rule movement, and he gargled with a word like 'manly' which had recently been coined by the Christian Socialists (*The Manliness of Christ,* Tom Hughes, 1879).

So when I found his name connected with the great Dublin scandal, I felt protective of my great-great-grandfather. I loved my own grandfather, and this was his grandfather – though they never actually met. I found I was even a little nervous, on behalf of my genes, about what I would find out. But equally, it seemed to me that he needed to be brought in from the cold. Whatever he did, he didn't deserve to have his only memorial on earth just the top of his head torn from a photo in the family album. But to bring him in from the cold, I had to know how he had been involved, and Dublin papers revealed little more than the fact that a warrant had been issued for his arrest.

*

This was not a generation where bankers worked long hours. In *The Dubliners* a generation after this, James Joyce wrote about a cashier in a private bank, coming in from Chapelizod by train every morning. "At midday he went to Dan Burke's and took his lunch – a bottle of beer and a small trayful of arrowroot biscuits," wrote Joyce. "At four o'clock he was set free. He dined in an eating house in George's Street ... where there was a certain plain honesty about the bill of fare."

This was a world where even the cashiers left work at teatime, and Richard Boyle was no cashier. He would go home and dress for his evenings out. By the time Joyce was writing, Boyle, Low, Murray and Co. was also one of only two remaining private banks in Ireland.

It isn't quite clear where the family lived by the time these events took place. They certainly lived at Milltown House, on the southern edge of Dublin next to Dublin Bay, but this seems to have been sold together with its outbuildings and their contents and a "serviceable donkey", in the summer of 1879 (to some nuns). Both Richard and his father were listed at various times as living above the bank in 35 College Green, a four-storey Georgian terraced house. There may have been living quarters there, but it isn't clear whether this was also the family home, with his wife Alice and his children (Helen, Olive, Alexander and Charles – Ernest died a few days after birth). More likely, they lived at his father's home at 12 Earlsfort Terrace, next to what is now the Royal University, in one of the white stuccoed Georgian terraced homes.

Either way, he seems to have taken a full part in the endless round of dinner parties in the Dublin ascendancy, coming home by hansom cab late at night. We catch glimpses of him at the Mayor of Dublin's receptions – with 'Miss

Boyle', perhaps the teenage Helen, perhaps his unmarried sister. There was a compelling *joie de vivre* about the upper circle of Unionists in those days, at dinner in each other's houses, discussing politics in the dying days of second Gladstone administration – the threat from Joseph Chamberlain and the menace of the Parnellites.

There is a scene in the James Joyce story 'The Dead', in *The Dubliners*, which describes one of these middle class Dublin dinners, in great detail, with the quadrilles, the semi-formal speeches, the piano in the next room and the leather bound song book:

"A fat brown goose lay at one end of the table and at the other end, on a bed of creased paper strewn with sprigs of parsley, lay a great ham, stripped of its outer skin and peppered over with crust crumbs, a neat paper frill round its shin and beside this was a round of spiced beef. Between these rival ends ran parallel lines of side-dishes: two little minsters of jelly, red and yellow; a shallow dish full of blocks of blancmange and red jam, a large green leaf-shaped dish with a stalk-shaped handle, on which lay bunches of purple raisins and peeled almonds, a companion dish on which lay a solid rectangle of Smyrna figs, a dish of custard topped with grated nutmeg, a small bowl full of chocolates and sweets wrapped in gold and silver papers and a glass vase in which stood some tall celery stalks. In the centre of the table there stood, as sentries to a fruit-stand which upheld a pyramid of oranges and American apples, two squat old-fashioned decanters of cut glass, one containing port and the other dark sherry. On the closed square piano a pudding in a huge yellow dish lay in waiting and behind it were three squads of bottles of stout and ale and minerals, drawn up according to the colours of their uniforms, the first two black, with brown and red labels, the third and smallest squad white, with transverse green sashes..."

That was the world of Richard Boyle's evenings, and presumably also those of his wife and two eldest daughters, now in their teenage years, and of the innumerable Boyle cousins living in Dublin at the time. We can imagine the dinner table discussions, about the imminent widening of the franchise, the explosion in Krakatoa (1883) and the ongoing siege of Khartoum (from March 1884), where General Gordon was holding out in the Sudan. Or perhaps gossip about Ellen Terry or Lily Langtry, or even Oscar Wilde in those early days of his fame (Lily Langtry was a protégé of Henry Labouchère's mistress, Henrietta Hodson). The conversation in *The Dubliners* was all about visiting Italian opera, and we know that what these dinners found most compelling in those days was music.

That was the conversation after dinner; that was the entertainment by gaslight afterwards. These were the great days of Gilbert and Sullivan. We can imagine these Unionist Dubliners, in that fateful year of 1884, around each other's pianos, testing out the new sheet music from *Iolanthe* or *The Pirates of Penzance* – Gilbert was even then writing *The Mikado* – perhaps joining in the Policeman's Chorus around the piano before their carriages arrived. Unfortunately, the term 'musical' was distorted with innuendo by the trial.

Even while the courtroom drama was continuing, the press continued to speculate about the whereabouts of the other people who should have been in the dock:

"A justice of the peace flying from justice is not altogether a reputable sight," said the *Nation* on 9 August:

"Mr Richard Boyle, a stockbroker and banker of Dublin – a gentleman who has, or at all events had, the right of attaching the letters J.P. to his name, is just now alleged to be in this position. Anticipating that a warrant would be issued for his arrest in connection with the Dublin scandals, Mr Boyle took his departure some weeks ago, it is said, secretly for places unknown."

It was probably to allay this kind of speculation that the family let it be known that he was definitely no longer in Dublin, in the statement that he was now in Spain that originally sent me down this peculiar path. He was removed from the lists of magistrates shortly afterwards.

*

Again by accident, that I found the clues I had been looking for in the Belfast papers, and suddenly a number of key elements fell into place. The few snippets there led me to a full account of the trial of Albert de Fernandez, the army surgeon, which took place after Cornwall had been acquitted. And here also I met the key figure of the trials, in a sense, face to face.

I had failed to understand how long the trials had continued, and the clues in the Belfast papers took me to *Freeman's Journal,* the moderate nationalist broadsheet, for 22 August 1884. And here finally, the situation had changed. The trials were grinding on, with little effect. Only three had been found guilty so far and the whole force of the law bore down on Pillar, and there in the witness box is the main source of evidence for a now reluctant crown prosecutor: the twenty-one year-old Malcolm Johnston.

Johnston was not by any means poor. His father was a successful baker, and founder of the company Johnston, Mooney & O'Brien, which made cakes. Johnston himself had been at school in Hamburg for a year, and while he was there he had met a well-connected English MP who had introduced him to Kirwan. He was then fifteen and had been involved with Kirwan in some kind of sexual encounter at the Gaiety Theatre. He had been to Trinity College, Dublin, and was then educated somewhere in Reading. He was one of the witnesses who the detective Meiklejohn had pinned down in London. He had also been a friend of most of the defendants, including Gustavus Cornwall, who had remarked about him: "what a pretty girl". Johnston, educated by a private tutor, was the lynchpin of the prosecution.

Now, he stood defiantly to give evidence. There was none of the broken, miserable or cautious witnesses who had gone before. Johnston was becoming immune to the pressure. He dressed to demonstrate he was rising above the fray, in a long overcoat with fur cuffs and collar. He wore patent leather boots and sported an impressive waxed moustache.

He swaggered as he stood there. But he failed to strike the right note of confidence to the court, as he was asked by the prosecution about his nickname: Lady Constance Clyde. Why? Because he lived in Clyde Street, with his father. It transpired that the man who had given him the name was a curate at Donnybrook, the Rev Thomas Dancer Hutchinson. Where was he, asked the judge? It seemed that he had left home in a hurry.

"Is he one of the parties involved in these matters?" asked the judge, rhetorically. Another friend of theirs who had also gone was a Roman Catholic priest, Fr Paul Keogh. Malcolm Johnston also turned out to be a cousin of one of the other defendants, distillery employee Johnston Little.

In the course of his cross-examination, he explained how he had been accosted by Fernandez in Stephen's Green Park, on the bridge in the People's Garden. Fernandez had asked him whether there were "any fish in the sea". Quite what transpired after that was not clear, but some kind of relationship grew up between them and they had gone on holiday together and stayed three weeks in the Victoria Hotel in Killarney. After that, Johnston had been promised a gold ring like the one Fernandez wore.

The gold ring was the crux of the case, and not a very good one. Fernandez had bought it in London and had engraved on it the words: "In memoriam, Juan to Mally, 14 June 1883".

Fernandez claimed that, in fact, that he wore his own ring as a memorial to his mother, and that she had died on that date.

Then, as far as I was concerned, the critical information: Fernandez had introduced him to Sankey, who was not explained. Was there anyone else, he was asked?

"Yes, to Mr Richard Boyle, the banker".

At last, I had some kind of clue about what my ancestor had been accused of. They had first met, it transpired, in Richard's offices in 35 College Green and "we became intimate", said Johnston.

So there was the central piece of information. Richard Boyle had fallen for this young man, and – if the Fernandez case was anything to go by – had given him presents. We shall never find out exactly what the evidence was against him, because – as we know – Richard escaped before he could be arrested. But when he heard what happened next, he might have wished he had risked staying.

The press, and probably also the court, were coy about exactly what Johnston and Fernandez were accused of doing, and by admitting it and giving evidence in this way – presumably as a result of intense pressure from Meiklejohn and O'Brien's lawyers – he was putting himself at risk. What did you think you were doing, he was asked? Johnston replied that he had no idea that what he was doing was a crime for which he could get penal servitude for life.

Why then did he sign a statement drawn up my Meiklejohn admitting to being party to unnatural crimes? Once again, the reluctance of the prosecutors to spell out what they meant had undermined their case. Johnston wriggled, his confidence faltering for a moment, and said he did he didn't know the meaning of the term 'unnatural crime'.

Fernandez was being skillfully defended by John Gibson QC, and Gibson clearly felt it was necessary to talk up the seriousness of the charges and the consequences of a guilty verdict:

"This man, if he was a man of honour, must feel that in his position in the dock, that it would have been better for him if he had never been born, than that he should be subjected to a charge in which – if he had been convicted – he would leave the court for the company of convicts for the rest of his natural life, condemned and blasted in his own reputation and ruined in his family, some of whom were present and actually listening to the painful details of this case."

Gibson's impassioned speech tore away at the lack of evidence, drawing applause from the public gallery – the public mood was clearly shifting. Then the judge brought the police prosecutor, Sergeant Hemphill, into the witness box. "Where is the corroboration?" he asked. After all, you could hardly just take Malcolm Johnston's word for it that sodomy had taken place.

"The corroboration is the ring," said the prosecutor.

"And I say it is no corroboration," said Dowse.

The jury were not out for long. The foreman proclaimed Fernandez not guilty and confirmed that it was the verdict of them all. "Yes," he said, "and we would like to say that there is not a stain on his character." Johnston Little was also discharged because the evidence against him also relied on his cousin's testimony and this now seemed unreliable.

"That is very satisfactory," said the judge, and in those words you can hear the sigh of relief of the protestant ascendancy. Another attempt to malign the ruling class of Dublin had been trounced. Another challenge to rule by landowners had been deflected: only a couple of the defendants, so far, had been found guilty and one was a Quaker of Spanish extraction. It was all "very satisfactory".

But, as we shall see, there were people in mainland Britain who did not find it satisfactory at all, one of them a Liberal MP and fervent friend and ally of Parnell and the Irish Nationalists called Henry Labouchère.

*

Now we reach the lynchpin of the story, at least as far as we are concerned. Richard Boyle was far from being the only pillar of respectability caught up in what was coming to be known as the 'Dublin Scandals'. As many as 30 names were on the list of "other people who were to be dragged down" and passed to the judge during the trial. Rumours began to circulate about whose names these might be. There were high-profile resignations among the officers of the Royal Irish Fusiliers. One person who left home suddenly was Charles Fitzgerald of Dalkey, whose name had been mentioned during the libel trial. His brother was taken in for questioning by mistake.

By the following weekend, July 19/20, the docks were heaving with detectives, trying to recognise potential defendants and witnesses and preventing them from leaving the country. But, by then, Richard Boyle had already gone. He left Dublin by sea some time on Tuesday 15 July.

We don't know the circumstances, whether he was alone in the decision or whether he consulted his wife or other members of the family. We don't know what he took with him, or whether he believed he would ever return. His son twelve-year-old son Alexander must have been due back from school that weekend. We don't know whether he said goodbye to him or his other children. Nor do we know, as family tradition suggests, whether he really went in disguise wearing a false nose.

But we do know something about his departure. Only three passenger ships left Dublin that day. Two were ferries to Holyhead which would not have guaranteed escape, and risked trapping him in England within reach of the police. He almost certainly took a cab late in the day, having organised as much money and valuables as he could carry with him, dressed in his oldest clothes – perhaps with a battered hat pulled down low over his head – and headed for Dublin's North Wall. He then caught the 7pm sailing for the City of Dublin Steam Packet

Co., a steam paddle steamer heading for Liverpool. At Liverpool the next morning, he booked a passage on the P&O mail boat to Cadiz.

And there the trail runs cold. He must have spent three days in cholera quarantine, because those were the regulations for arrivals from the UK. But we know nothing about why he chose Spain, but the most likely reason was that it was the quickest destination available when he arrived in Liverpool. It seems unlikely that he intended to stay there, or that his family should join him there. We don't know where he went, though it may well have been Madrid.

We know that, as he arrived at North Wall in the late evening sunlight, the evening papers were reporting not just Cornwall's arrest but also French's. We also know that the authorities issued a warrant for Boyle's arrest, but not for some days afterwards. The *Evening Telegraph* reported on Saturday – after the bulk of arrests had been completed – that only one other warrant had been issued and the police "do not hesitate to express their doubts as to the probability of the person concerned being arrested".

There is a kind of lassitude about this, a fatalism about the police response, which almost implies that they deliberately waited to issue the warrant. Their fear may have been that, by arresting someone so well-known in Dublin's business world, they would escalate the scandal uncontrollably. There was the same gentlemanly approach taken to Oscar Wilde's arrest eleven years later: the magistrate is supposed to have timed the warrant to take effect after the boat train had left London (he didn't, in fact).

*

The case was over, Unionism had been identified with homosexuality, and it stayed identified for a generation. When the Irish crown jewels disappeared from Dublin Castle 1907, the press was quick to point the finger at a homosexual coterie who had run the business of Irish heraldry there. The case had also lit the touchpaper of an explosive moral panic on both sides of the Irish Sea, where 'right-thinking people' began to demand action. "A deep burning shame mantles the cheek of Ireland," said the *Derry Journal*.

The scene was set for the ruin of Oscar Wilde exactly a decade later. No doubt he remembered Gustavus Cornwall's escape in identical circumstances after a failed libel action as he delayed in the Cadogan Hotel before his arrest. Cornwall had been acquitted so perhaps that is why he delayed.

There was also carping in the press about the incompetent handling of the prosecution case. "We may reasonably suspect," said the *Nation* on 30 August, "that Mr Richard Boyle, ex J.P., has been watching from his self-imposed exile in Spain, the course matters have taken, and that as a consequence he will shortly return to his residence in Dublin. It is more than probable that if any definite knowledge of the way in which the government intended to manage the prosecution had gone abroad before the trial commenced, Mr

Boyle would not have left home, and Mr Pillar would not have pleaded guilty."

But it was too late, of course. The damage was done, but the implications for those caught up in the panic were very far from being over. For the Unionists, Meiklejohn and O'Brien's solicitors had put the witnesses Taylor and Johnston into a state of such terror that they would have been prepared to swear to almost anything. For the Nationalists, the attempt to link Unionism with homosexuality would have far-reaching implications.

I still didn't really know the circumstances which caused my great-great-grandfather to run? But there was a clue in events that took place in Dublin the following summer.

Robert Farquharson, the colourful manager of Munster Bank in Dublin, jointly in charge of the Dame Street and College Green branches, had been siphoning off small amounts of money into his own account for years. But some time in the summer of 1884, after the resignation of the bank chairman, he began to withdraw very large amounts. The future of his bank was already in doubt by 1885, and early in July the shareholders called in accountants to wind it up. On Friday 24 July, the accountants discovered a peculiarity in the Dame Street branch accounts. The following day, they turned up more, amounting to more than £70,000. They confronted Farquharson, and he escaped the following afternoon, pursued by the police.

The collapse of Munster Bank was the last bank failure before the Irish banking crisis of 2009, so these events have been studied closely by historians, notably Cormac Ó Gráda in his 2001 paper 'Should the Munster Bank have been saved?'

Ó Gráda describes Farquharson as a bachelor, sharing 57 Leeson Park with an elderly servant and a gardener and hosting dinners for twenty or thirty several times a week, but almost every night in the weeks before his disappearance. The police newspaper *Hue and Cry* described him as "about 40 years old, 5 feet 9 inches high, dark hair, dark beard, whiskers and moustache, slightly tinged with gray, dark fresh complexion, good dark sparkling eyes, prominent teeth, average build, walks with a stoop, dressed in a gentlemanly style, generally wears a silk hat."

He was so prominent in the Dublin banking community that Charles McCarthy Collins dedicated his 1880 book *Law and Practice of Banking in Ireland* to him. He had a sizeable collection of jewellery and was a major speculator on the stock exchange. Ó Gráda continues:

"Farquharson was last spotted in Dublin on the platform of Amiens Street railway station. A friend who saw him there said that he travelled third class, and was wearing a low, shabby, jerry hat. Stories of subsequent sightings conflicted; in one version he took the Belfast train but alighted at Dunleer near Dundalk; in another he made for Tralee to board a sailing ship bound for Baltimore in the United States, in another he had been traced to Ardrossan, in yet another he was arrested in Queenstown. Several travellers on Wednesday's Drogheda-Liverpool steamer spoke of a strange gentleman with only a brown paper parcel for luggage. Spain was mentioned as one of his likely destinations, but another rumour had him reaching Amsterdam in early August, and converting most of his money into diamonds there. In either place he would have been safe from extradition proceedings. The offer of a reward of £500 for his arrest proved of no avail; in Ireland he was never seen."

Farquharson must have known Richard Boyle well. They managed banks at the same address and they were both closely involved in the Dublin stock exchange. Both disappeared in similar ways exactly a year apart, both ending up apparently in Spain. One report suggests that Farquharson was wearing a false nose, which is another link. If it was Farquharson and not Boyle who wore the false nose, then the family has confused their stories. I decided there must have been some reason for that confusion. There must have been some other connection between their separate flights from the law.

Munster Bank was wound up and found, to everyone's surprise, actually to have been solvent. But it transpired that Farquharson's £70,000 – a huge sum (at least £6 million in today's money) – had been taken out only since the previous year, since the Cornwall trial. He had been stealing small sums since he had been based in Cork, but for some reason he needed to increase these sums, and enormously increase his own risk. It is quite possible that the £70,000 and the trials were actually connected, and that the reason for his recklessness was that he was being blackmailed in connection with the scandal – probably by Meiklejohn.

If he was being blackmailed, then you have to wonder whether the same thing had happened to Richard Boyle. If one banker was being blackmailed by Meiklejohn, then why not his colleague upstairs at the same address? It may be that Meiklejohn had kept the names of the wealthy bankers in reserve, hoping to earn some extra money out of the affair, aware that his chances of employment after this were scarce. It would explain such an early escape.

All this is circumstantial evidence, and sometimes not even that, but taken together it does begin to provide a picture of what may have happened, and all I could do was imagine the gaps. This is what I therefore believe took place.

Farquharson's sumptuous dinner parties had become almost nightly after the Dublin Scandals, but there was a reason for that. The Dublin gay community, though it hardly regarded itself in this way, had nowhere to hide and nowhere to meet. These dinners were the alternative – not all of them, but many of them – where members of the city's gay community could meet each other where there was no risk of a public glimpse. They were paid for regularly by the wealthier members but attended, not just by them, but by other trusted people as well – as they had been for some years.

They were also open to a wider group of people, all men, who found the conversation liberating and enjoyed the camp repartee and perhaps the promise of something else. After the fateful summer of 1884 , this was the only safe places for this kind of event – the homosexual brothels had been closed and the ferocious public reception was echoing in their frightened ears. Before the summer of 1884, Farquharson's parties took place as they did later, though only three or four times a week, and the music – and again I have to guess – was provided by the Munster Bank cashier with the "beautiful voice", Alfred McKiernan.

I believe that Richard used to attend some of these parties, though probably not very often. But his attendance led him to some kind of involvement, originally with the army surgeon Albert de Fernandez, who shared his interest also in public health. Fernandez, as we know, introduced him to Malcolm Johnston, with his boots and waxed moustache.

Those who attended those parties occasionally included some of the most powerful names in Ireland and there was a reluctance on the part of the authorities to widen their inquiry to include them. But there was the evidence. It was in the hands of Meiklejohn and his fearsome solicitors, and Meiklejohn could not ignore this source of revenue. The potential sources of lucrative employment for a disgraced policeman were few and far between, and he needed to think of his retirement.

From the moment it was apparent that Johnston was going to be a witness in the Cornwall libel action, Richard Boyle must have begun to fear the worst. His nervous weekly perusal of *United Ireland* – not a paper he enjoyed reading – turned up no evidence that could possibly link his name to this terrifying spectacle of public rage and disgust. But he must have known that his name was on the list of 30 and known why. He must have bumped into other people named and discussed possible options before them, without perhaps revealing why he was so nervous.

Throughout that awful weekend of July 12/13, as the evidence of mob rage began to become apparent, the main question on his mind – above almost anything else – was whether the government would be forced to act. Then late on Sunday night at the family home, the late evening sun having now finally disappeared into the western suburbs of Dublin, there was a knock on the front door.

Terrified, he came out of his study. Had the mob arrived already at his home?

"A Mr Meiklejohn to see you, Sir. He says you will know what it's about." The gaslight flickered on the face of a poker-faced man with a wide moustache removing a bowler hat.

"Thank you. Will you show him in? Mr Meiklejohn, I know you by reputation."

"Thank you, Mr Boyle. That saves me some explanation about my visit. My apologies for the lateness of the hour."

"And what is your business exactly, Mr Meiklejohn?"

"If you will forgive me, Sir, but what I have to say needs to be in strictest confidence. I need to speak with you alone, if you don't mind. For your own good as well as mine..."

"Very well," said the master of the house, a cold shiver of fear running down his neck at this naked threat. "Follow me. I am at your service."

Perhaps, as he watched Meiklejohn's silhouette disappearing into the night, he briefly considered paying the huge sum demanded. Meiklejohn was in no doubt what the price of bankers was in Dublin. But this seemed in some ways an even more risky undertaking. Was his name not on the list of 30, after all? Could Meiklejohn actually guarantee safety from prosecution – when he had already been warned that his name was the subject of tittle-tattle in the bars along the Liffey? No, there really was only one option. If the worst came to the worst.

For such a political man, the horror of what his own mistake would do to the cause he represented weighed particularly heavily. And then there was his family...

Did he arrive for work in College Green the next morning? Did he consider remonstrating with Malcolm, holed up under police protection in a small city centre hotel? Did he discuss matters with Farquharson? Or did he draft a letter to his wife and children and try and make a list of assets that he could remove at a moment's notice from the country?

One look at the evening papers on Monday convinced him. Cornwall had been arrested and the crackdown had begun. There was no choice. He had to leave, and before Meiklejohn could make good his threat to lay the evidence against him before the police. Early the next morning, he told his wife and daughters – Alexander was not at home and Charles was too young – and the picture of their appalled and sickened faces stayed with him all the way to the dockside at North Wall, across the Irish Sea and beyond.

Much of the rest of the story we can hardly imagine. The flight of Robert Farquharson a year later became confused in the minds of his family – the false nose – because they knew that Farqhuarson had arranged those musical dinners where the damage had been done. Perhaps they also knew he had been threatened by Meiklejohn but had paid up, and had helped ruin the Munster Bank as a result. Perhaps there was some other connection with the Munster Bank that I am unaware of.

*

So ended the Dublin Scandal, now largely forgotten. It burst onto the political scene in Ireland in a traditional manner – the way resurgent political opponents drag down their ruling elite using sexual accusation. It established a precedent that was soon copied by the other side. In Belfast, the independent Conservative MP Edward de Cobain had enraged both sides, including the Royal Irish Constabulary, whose conduct he had criticised after the Belfast riots of 1886. He was the next victim, tried for gross indecency in his home in the Ormeau Road.

But it also had the opposite effect that was intended. Because in mainland Britain, the main element of the whole affair that the chattering classes remembered was that gay sex was somehow peculiarly Irish. "Where did you commence committing these crimes?" Malcolm Johnston was asked in 1884.

"In Dublin," he replied.

"And you brought the practice with you to London."

It was no more than a simple statement of fact, but it was adopted in England as an explanation. The main witness in

London's Cleveland Street scandal in 1889 was a male prostitute – a 'Mary Ann' – calling himself 'Dublin Jack'. Oscar Wilde was accused of bringing his 'practices' from Trinity College, Dublin, to Oxford. Paradoxically, in the popular imagination, Dublin became the source of the scourge.

Those in Westminster who had most studied Irish affairs also took up the cudgels and looked for a way of making these prosecutions a little more effective. The opportunity to do so was presenting itself in the culmination of a successful campaign for state involvement in sexual morality.

4

"I consider it a disgrace that such matter should ever be allowed to be published in any newspaper that calls itself respectable. I have taken care that my girls do not read such filth, and I hope that every parent has done the same."
Letter to the *Pall Mall Gazette*, 9 July 1885

William Thomas Stead was the red-bearded, campaigning editor of the *Pall Mall Gazette*, one of the foremost journalists of the age, and a pioneer in the field of investigative journalism. In the process of his most famous campaign, he found himself on trial for abduction and indecent assault, and was sentenced to a month's imprisonment. It seems paradoxical to us, but would not have done at the time, that the events around Stead's imprisonment were also the moment that the concept of 'gross indecency' made its appearance in British law. This was not because of Stead, but because of his unreliable ally Henry Labouchère.

It was also no coincidence that the first great feminist campaign, known to its detractors as the 'purity' campaign, had just come to fruition under the leadership of the pioneering campaigner Josephine Butler. The controversial Contagious

Diseases Acts had been suspended, and the successful campaigners were now pressing home their advantage.

Stead and Butler were important players in the prevailing mood in the 1880s and 1890s, which was regarded at the time as a search for purity, but could equally be described as a search for authenticity. On the one hand, there was growing energy behind the campaign to make visible those sexual abuses which Victorian society had preferred to brush aside. On the other hand, there were those who tapped into the same spirit, and saw it as demanding a new openness and truth to self – like Edward Carpenter, the gay pioneer, then living with the labourer George Merrill he met on the train in Sheffield in 1891. Or Oscar Wilde and the aesthetic pioneers who regarded the truth rather differently. Both sides in this dialogue of the deaf regarded each other with some horror. Both fuelled the emerging idea that British society was hurtling towards a kind of sick decadence. This is how the great historian of the Victorian age, G. M. Young, put it:

"Fundamentally, what failed in the late Victorian age, and its flashy Edwardian epilogue, was the Victorian public, once so alert, so masculine, and so responsible. Compared with their fathers, the men of that time were ceasing to be a ruling or a reasoning stock; the English mind sank towards easily excited, easily satisfied, state of barbarism and childhood."

That has always been the reaction of the middlebrow, who regard periods of peace and relative prosperity as breeding indolence and luxury. It was a period of great social and technological change, from women cyclists to motor cars and cinemas, and this was the reaction. The American critic Karl Beckson describes the prevailing attitude to the final decade of the nineteenth century as "the the decline or decay of such phenomena as cricket, genius, war, classical quotations, romance, marriage, faith, bookselling and even canine fidelity".

Even dogs were descending into decadence. The horror! And he blamed the rapid changes in society for it, "with much talk of the New Drama, the New Woman, the New Journalism, the New Imperialism, the New Criticism, the New Hedonism, the New Paganism." The idea came together most forcefully in a book by Max Simon Nordau called *Degeneration*, published that fateful year of 1895 – the year that the purity campaigners, the Irish Nationalists, the middle class fear of degeneration and the mob all came together in a poisonous combination, which led to the moment of fear which began this book. And it crushed Wilde's brief cult of decadence at the same time.

What Labouchère's change in the law tried to do was not to bear down on a type of person, or even a psychological phenomenon. That language had not yet emerged. The target was a form of behaviour which seemed to signify a decadent mindset. It was driven by a fear that luxury had made society effeminate. And if the Dublin Scandal provided the spark, the fuse was set by the campaign against child sex abuse – and we have to remember that some of Wilde's young men were under seventeen. Malcolm Johnston was fifteen when he met

Gustavus Cornwall, so he would now be entitled to be described as a 'victim'.

*

Josephine Butler was an important figure, like Stead, who linked the worlds of Christian evangelical campaigning and the emerging feminist movement. She was to pass on her mantel to Millicent Fawcett, her biographer, who took the campaign for women's suffrage through to victory in 1918. But she had begun with a courageous stance against the Contagious Diseases Acts in the 1860s, when the government attempted to clamp down on venereal disease in garrison or naval towns, which gave wide powers to local officials to arrest women suspected of being prostitutes and to lock them up for three months if they were found to be infected.

As the campaign progressed, Josephine Butler came under increasing attack from the establishment, mainly because of the idea among the wealthier men in Parliament that their sons should be allowed to experiment sexually – though that is not how they put it – without the fear of disease. Her response made her a critical figure in the gender wars to come, because she did not fall back on appeals to Christian abstinence, but for equality before the law. "Let your laws be put by force," she said, "but let them be for male as well as female, and let them include civilian gentlemen."

It was a brave line to take and a revolutionary one. She came under increasing public attack, on occasions only escaping from mobs by the skin of her teeth, smuggled out of the back doors of draughty halls. It was also a long and ultimately successful campaign and, after the Contagious Diseases Acts were suspended in 1883, the next step was to look more closely at the brothels and inevitably this led to fears about child trafficking. Her partnership with Stead on this issue led to the drafting of the government's half-hearted response, a bill designed to raise the age of sexual consent from thirteen.

This had been introduced to Parliament in 1881 when the anti-vice campaigner Benjamin Scott asked Lord Granville to protect young girls being sent to the continent as white slaves. Granville persuaded the House of Lords to set up a committee to investigate and they made a series of recommendations, which – under pressure from Butler and Stead – were drafted into the Criminal Law Amendment Bill.

The bill passed the House of Lords in 1883 and again in 1884, but languished in the Commons, which consistently refused to pass it. The Dublin Scandal was done and dusted before the bill was modified again in the spring of 1885 and reintroduced by the Earl of Dalhousie, when it was savaged by the Earl of Milltown for "making criminals out of honest men".

But the Lords stood firm and passed it again, only to have it run into major apathy in the Commons. The Whitsun recess was approaching and there was opposition from Liberals like the Stockport MP Charles Hopwood, another supporter of Irish home rule, who was afraid that the increased powers of the police would be misused. No vote was taken and it looked as if the bill would simply be abandoned for want of support.

A desperate Josephine Butler swung into action. Benjamin Scott also went to Stead to see what could be done, and he had an idea in the back of his mind. The following day, Stead went to see a former head of Scotland Yard's Criminal Investigation Department, Sir Howard Vincent – who was among those campaigning for tougher laws against homosexual behaviour. Vincent told him some lurid stories about child prostitution. Stead followed up with a series of clandestine interviews with pimps, prostitutes, rescue workers and prison chaplains. But he needed something else that was capable of capturing public imagination.

As late spring turned to early summer 1885, when *The Mikado* was first playing at London's Savoy Theatre (since March), and General Gordon was lying fresh in his tomb in Khartoum, he met a retired madam called Rebecca Jarrett who told him about a thirteen-year-old girl called Eliza Armstrong whose alcoholic mother needed money. Here was Stead's story and it turned out to be one of the most explosive pieces of investigative journalism in the century.

Jarrett told the mother that the girl was going to serve as a maid, but believed the mother understood that she was selling her daughter into prostitution. Jarrett and Stead then took Eliza to a midwife who gave her chloroform to examine her and to make sure she was a virgin, and it was this examination that Stead would eventually face trial for taking part in. Eliza was then handed over to Bramwell Booth of the Salvation Army –

key players in Stead's campaign – who spirited her out of the country to safety in France.

Stead's frenetic activities were dictated to relays of note-takers while he paced his office with an ice pack on his head. The resulting articles were published under the title 'The Maiden Tribute of Modern Babylon', revealing that young girls could be bought on the streets from eleven years old. The first of these editions took up six pages and included the headline 'Five pounds for a virgin warranted pure'. He also included some trenchant criticisms of MPs for failing to act to tackle the abuse.

The Home Secretary Sir William Harcourt contacted Stead the following day and asked him to stop publishing the articles. Stead agreed – he was running short of paper thanks to the demand – on condition that the Criminal Law Amendment Bill was carried. Harcourt could give no such guarantee so Stead ordered his printers to carry on printing until the paper ran out. Booksellers W. H. Smith refused to stock the issue on the grounds of prurience, but the Salvation Army volunteered to distribute copies instead. Meanwhile, the beleaguered MPs began demanding that Stead should be prosecuted under the obscenity laws.

As June passed on to July, Stead kept up his campaign on two fronts, partly to raise the age of sexual consent. He had also been backing a bid by the new Society for the Prevention of Cruelty to Children, the forerunner of the NSPCC to pass an 'oath clause', so that child victims of sexual assault under twelve could give evidence in court. When MPs voted against, Stead published their names.

The first installment of 'The Maiden Tribute' had been published on 6 July 1885 and sold an unprecedented million and a half copies Three days later, the government caved in and promised to act, and even then it was hardly enough. As many as 400,000 people had signed a Salvation Army petition demanding that the bill should be passed and the age of consent raised.

The House of Commons was by then in a holiday mood, partly enraged by the pressure being piled on them, partly amused by the peculiar anger of some of their number. The cricketing Tory MP George Cavendish-Bentinck asked the Home Secretary whether he was aware of "a certain paper publishing objectionable matter through the metropolis, and whether any means of subjecting the author and publishers if this objectionable publicity to criminal proceedings?" For days afterwards, MPs fell about laughing whenever Cavendish-Bentinck came into the Commons chamber, shouting "pity the poor old fornicator".

Cavendish-Bentinck, fornicator or not, was a long-standing ally of the equally individualist radical MP Henry Labouchère. And when the government's business managers put the Criminal Law Amendment Bill back into the schedule before the summer recess, both men's first reactions had been to undermine it – for different reasons perhaps, but both men opposed police involvement in people's private lives and regarded this as a thin end of the wedge. That had been their attitude last time it had been debated, but the background was now different. The Dublin Scandal had unfolded since the bill had last been debated. The issues seemed unrelated, but both involved young people and prostitution, and anyway Dublin Castle and the back streets of London had become linked in the minds of some party managers. Especially those with an interest in Irish issues, like Labouchère who had followed the events closely, the only one of the London editors to do so. "The Irish members cannot be blamed for making a good deal of capital out of the recent disclosures anent (*sic*) the castle employés," he wrote on 31 July, before the trials, focussing attention on Cornwall and French, in the pay of the administration at Dublin Castle:

"I dare say there are some honourable and honest men amongt them. But the flock seems a black – a very black – one; and the white sheep are rare – very rare: indeed a more foul and scabby set of sheep never exercised sway in any land."

It was at this point, in the high summer of 1885, that Labouchère, now one of two Liberal MPs for Northampton and a tireless supporter of Irish nationalist issues, decided to intervene.

*

Labouchère had inherited a great deal of money and in turns infuriated and charmed his Liberal colleagues in the House of

Commons. He always dressed like a tramp. It was said that you could smell him coming upstairs to his own newspaper office. He was a great friend of some of the most outspoken and ego-fuelled characters of the age, the pioneer socialist H. M. Hyndman, the artist James McNeil Whistler and the reforming future admiral Jackie Fisher. He was famous both for his cynicism and for his own very high opinion of his own abilities – he was constantly in a state of rage that his requests for preferment were being ignored by the Foreign Office, his former employers. He had first came to the public eye during the Franco-Prussian War in 1871, writing despatches from Paris under siege, and then under the Communards, for the Liberal newspaper the *Daily News*.

He used the fortune he had inherited to launch his own weekly newspaper *Truth* in 1877, with the task of hunting down frauds – political and consumer – imposing his opinions on political debate and trying to abolish the House of Lords. He was elected in 1865 and lost his seat shortly afterwards: when he came back in 1880, he promptly enraged his new colleagues by launching a personal attack on Benjamin Disraeli when they were supposed to be paying tribute to him to mark his death.

"Beware of Labby," Harcourt told Joseph Chamberlain. "He talks to everybody, writes to everybody and betrays everybody."

Labouchère had become a familiar, shambolic sight around Westminster, famous for his cynicism, particularly in his alliance with Cavendish-Bentinck to undermine the

Criminal Law Amendment Act. This was partly because Stead and the *Pall Mall Gazette* were the arch-rivals in investigative journalism with *Truth,* and Labouchère was irritated by the success of 'The Maiden Tribute'. But it was also because, despite – or possibly because – of his libertarian radicalism, Labouchère was also a great hater: and he particularly hated Jews, feminists and homosexuals. He carried on a long fued with W. S. Gilbert ("Oh it's tough on Labouchère," went a song from *His Excellency*). He was a friend and ally of Parnell and he agreed with Parnell, and did so passionately, that it was a pity the Dublin authorities had been unable to prosecute the offenders with greater vigour the previous summer.

Oddly for a man who has given his name to the criminalisation of gay sex, Labouchère was at the time living out of wedlock with the Irish actress Henrietta Hodson, a friend of Oscar Wilde's, who he had met when he was involved in launching the new Queen's Theatre in London. They married when her husband died in 1887.

In other ways, Labouchère was far-sighted. He was strongly in favour of home rule for Ireland, of old age pensions – even of a minimum wage – and history was on his side in all these opinions. But his contemporaries tended to bracket them sometimes with his peculiarities: he drank skimmed milk in preference to alcohol. And despite his loathing of homosexual activity, he was opposed to the state legislating on sexual morality. He would stand by the Chelsea MP Sir Charles Dilke after the so-called three-in-a-bed scandal in 1886, and was Gladstone's intermediary with the wronged husband, the new

MP for Lanarkshire North East, Donald Crawford. Stead attacked him after this for "cynical immorality". Labouchère replied that he would "rather be cynically immoral than pruriently pure".

His tactics were simple. First, he attacked the bill for its muddled amendments. "The greatest care ought to be taken not to confound immorality with crime, not to over-run in the well-meaning confusion," he said, "... and not to play in the hands of the blackmailers." Even at the time, that was what his contemporaries were to accuse him of. Next, he and Cavendish-Bentinck tried to confuse the issue themselves by trying to raise the age of female sexual consent as far as twenty-one, aware that this would outlaw many apparently respectable aristocratic marriages. Having failed with that, they then tried for eighteen. The Commons eventually voted for sixteen.

It may have been Stead who changed his perspective on the bill. He wrote to Labouchère from prison some weeks later, after his conviction for the abduction of Eliza Armstrong, urging him to act on male prostitution, aware that *Truth* had been strong on the issue since the Dublin events. It can't have been the first communication between them on the subject.

The immediate effect of Stead's articles was his own arrest, as well as all those who had helped him 'buy' Eliza. His case came to trial in October after other papers had identified the mother and she had protested her innocence – and it transpired that, in any case, nobody had asked permission from the father. Nor were a succession of witnesses that Stead called to court to defend his motives, including the Archbishop of Canterbury, able to cut much ice. The case was proved. Bramwell Booth was acquitted, but Stead and his assistants were found guilty. He was sentenced to three months in Holloway Prison, which he claimed he enjoyed, editing the paper from gaol and relaxing in front of a fire in his cell. "Never had I a pleasanter holiday, a more charming season of repose," he used to say.

He wasn't the only journalist to have become obsessed with homosexuality. This was *Yokel's Preceptor*, a contemporary magazine, in the run-up to the debate, and it reveals that the public perception was beginning to shift from a horror about gay behaviour to a more twentieth century horror about a psychological type:

"The increase of these monsters in the shape of men,
commonly designated margeries, poofs etc., of late years, in
the great Metropolis, renders it necessary for the safety of the
public that they should be made known…Will the reader credit
it, but such is nevertheless the fact, that these monsters
actually walk the street the same as the whores, looking out for
a chance? Yes, the Quadrant, Fleet Street, Holborn, the Strand
etc., are actually thronged with them! Nay, it is not long since,
in the neighbourhood of Charing Cross, they posted bills in the
windows of several public houses, cautioning the public to
'Beware of Sods!'."

But the jubilation when the bill passed the Commons on the way to being law was widespread. Stead joined the Salvation Army for their victory parade in Hyde Park on 22 August. They had done what seemed impossible: at their third attempt, they had raised the age of sexual consent. It was an important achievement. The 'oath clause' proved to be important too. There was soon a flurry of prosecutions for sexual assaults on children and young people, made possible because children could now give evidence in court. But they were not high profile prosecutions of decadent aristocrats, as Stead had assumed. Those who ended up doing hard labour for assaulting children were, then as now, largely the working classes. Ten years later, the 1896 Criminal Statistics noted that "the growth of public sentiment with regard to sexual crime, of which the Criminal Law Amendment Act was one manifestation, is no doubt responsible for the more vigorous prosecution of offences."

It is strange, but perhaps not surprising, that these achievements were overshadowed by the one shift in the criminal law that the new bill was not intended to make – the criminalisation of all homosexual behaviour, even in public. Because, in the early hours of the morning of 7 August 1885, when the bill finally came back to the Commons, Labouchère had changed his mind. He put down a serious amendment. This is what Amendment 11 said:

"Any male person who, in public or private, commits, or is a party to the commission of, or procures or attempts to procure the commission of any male person of any act of gross indecency with another male person, shall be guilty of misdemeanour, and being convicted thereof shall be liable at the discretion of the court to be imprisoned for any term not exceeding two years, with or without hard labour."

It was the dead of night when Labouchère rose to move it, and he had made his preparations effectively, squaring the government whips, to make sure the clause would be accepted. It was an extremely short speech for such a far-reaching measure, explaining simply that his idea was simply to abolish the idea of any age of consent for this kind of 'assault'.

This is how Hansard minuted his brief speech:

"That was his Amendment, and the meaning of it was that at present any person on whom an assault of the kind here dealt with was committed must be under the age of 13, and the object with which he had brought forward this clause was to make the law applicable to any person, whether under the age of 13 or over that age. He did not think it necessary to discuss the proposal at any length, as he understood Her Majesty's government were willing to accept it. He, therefore, left it for the House and the government to deal with as might be thought best."

And that was that. The whole debate on the amendment took four minutes. Only one member spoke against the amendment. Berwick MP Charles Wharton questioned whether it bore any relation to the original purpose of the bill. The speaker said it didn't matter. There was also an intervention by the former attorney-general Sir Henry James, who said that the sentence needed to have a higher maximum, and he suggested two years (Labouchère had originally proposed seven years).

The journalist Frank Harris suggested later that Labouchère had moved the amendment to carry on bringing the new law into disrepute. But read the transcript of the debate and it is clear Labouchère was committed to what was happening, and in fact moved a second amendment shortly afterwards – to provide a mechanism to take children into the care of someone other than the parent who had abused them.

Whatever his motives, Labouchère may not have realised that this was the way his name was going to echo down history. Of all his work in Ireland and other radical causes, it was the Labouchère amendment and the criminalisation of gay sex that he would be remembered for.

5

"Not a year passes in England without somebody disappearing. Scandals used to lend charm, at least interest to a man. Now they crush him. And yours is a very nasty scandal."
Oscar Wilde, *An Ideal Husband*, Act 1

By the time Labouchère had moved his amendment, both Robert Farquharson and Richard Boyle were in Spain. Richard was unlikely to have intended to stay there. Perhaps the major cholera outbreak – 80,000 dead by the following year – encouraged him to move to Germany. Perhaps he always intended to go there, knowing that his daughter could study medicine there instead. Farquharson disappeared from history, but his death was reported in Dublin the following July, in 1886. Perhaps he succumbed to cholera. We don't know.

But we do know that the rest of the Boyle family arrived in Bonn-auf-Rhein in Germany some time later. For Richard's eldest daughter Helen, who had inherited his interest in health and was determined to become a doctor, removal from Dublin was a particularly bitter blow. She was seventeen in 1886 and, unusually for the great universities of Europe, Dublin was one of the few places which awarded medical degrees to women. It may be that Germany was chosen as some consolation for her, because there were places in Germany where it was possible to qualify as a doctor.

And there the story should come to a close, but we know it didn't. Family legend suggests that whatever it was "happened again", though whether this was just a romantic entanglement with a young man, or also a blackmail attempt, we don't know. Alice decided to leave her husband, and Richard gravely asked the children whether they would like to go with their mother or stay with him, and – without exception – they chose their mother. That may have been the bitterest blow of all. Again, we don't know. It seems likely that the basic raw material for blackmail had been collected in Dublin by Meiklejohn with a view to using it to pay the bills later – in which case the Labouchère amendment, now Section 11 of the Criminal Law Amendment Act, must have seemed a welcome extra weapon.

Either way, this marked the end of the Boyle family as a unit. Richard stopped paying for Alexander's education at Charterhouse, and Alice and the children moved to 46 Alma Vale, a quiet terraced street near Clifton Down Station in Bristol, where they could afford to send Alexander (and later Charles) to Clifton College as a day boy. He started there in September 1887 and stayed for two years. Helen had been at the Hohere Fochterschule in Bonn-auf-Rhein in Germany and maybe also in Brussels, but she followed her mother to Clifton. Then in July 1889, she was accepted into Elizabeth Garrett Anderson's London School of Medicine for Women.

Three years later she qualified as a doctor, and then spent a year in Brussels becoming a Doctor of Medicine.

She worked in London's East End, at a large psychiatric hospital outside Ilford and then at the Canning Town dispensary, before the move to Brighton in 1898 to begin her eminent career there with her own hospital in Hove. That same year, her father remains conspicuously absent from the photographs at her brother Alexander's wedding. Family tradition says that Richard's brother, Colonel Edward Boyle, provided a link between Richard and his family. In fact, there he is staying with them in Bristol on census day 1891. But, there also the trail seemed to go cold. The gulf was so complete that there is no memory in the family, back through the generations I have known, about what happened to him next.

*

But the trail isn't completely cold, and – having uncovered the secret about what he was supposed to have done in Dublin – I really wanted to somehow dig out the lesser secret of what happened next. If it was a lesser secret, or just something that had been forgotten.

There were two clues to start with. I knew he had died at the end of 1900, and – thanks to Helen Boyle's biographer, Emma Milliken, it became pretty clear that Richard had not stayed in Germany for long after his family had left. Around 1890, he came back to London. Emma Milliken wrote that he was believed to be running a glass factory in Canning Town, and certainly he was involved in some way with glass. Canning Town was a centre of glass manufacture, and the City Glass Bottle Company was founded there in 1890, and he may have been involved in some way perhaos as an investor. There was also a Richard Boyle running a shop in East London for most of the 1890s, at 28 Canning Town East Side , next to the glass manufacturers in Canning Town. Later the shop was at 28 Frederick Road, near Custom House.

This was intriguing, because it suggested that Helen had stayed in touch with her father after the split, keeping it secret perhaps to protect her mother. It makes no sense that they worked within a few streets of each other without knowing it.

But getting a copy of Richard Boyle's death certificate provided me with the first definite information. I was able to work backwards and discover that, by 1891, he was living in Camberwell, a suburb on the southern edge of London, and was describing himself as artist. Was that was a way of avoiding identifying himself as a banker? There is some evidence that he was, to start with at least, continuing with his old banking contacts in London. But he was, after all, a wanted man. He had to be careful.

Still, it felt exciting to find him, and rather extraordinary that – for most of the rest of his life – he was living within walking distance of my own home for twenty-five years in Norwood. Because there he was, in black and white, living at 8 Champion Grove, a whitewashed two-storey Georgian semi, which he owned. It probably had rather pompous white pillars on either side of the front door; it is hard to tell because numbers 8 and 10 Champion Grove were bombed in the Second World War and have been replaced by modern homes.

He described his occupation to the census official as 'artist on glass', which is so precise that it may well have referred to a specific job he was doing at the time. Note this was not 'artist *with* glass', and nor was it 'engraver'. One explanation was that he was involved in some way in the booming stained glass industry, not just for churches but in public buildings and ordinary homes, and that he was painting the figures and letters that went on top. The painted glass in the Camberwell Public Baths down the road is still there, and – since that was being painted in 1891– it is tempting to imagine him carrying out part of the commission.

I could almost visualise him at the opening of the baths in October 1892, pottering down there through the smog and horse dung, dodging the horse-drawn omnibuses with his friend Penrose – of whom more in a moment – to watch the local MPs, the Mayor of Camberwell and the architects and builders being piped in by the band of the First Surrey Rifles. Or watching what the local paper called the "interesting and pretty" display of swimming and floating by children from the local school.

But these were also the years when the successful stained glass specialists Lavers, Barraud and Westlake were making windows for St Giles', Camberwell, so perhaps he had become interested via the Arts and Crafts movement, then at its height. Perhaps, at the very least, he had on his desk Nathanial

Westlake's four volume *A History of Design in Painted Glass* (1891-4). On the other hand, if his artistry was related to bottles or, more likely, painting pictures on panes of glass, his energy may have been more focused on Canning Town.

Camberwell included some of the worst slums in London, down the Walworth Road, as well as the relatively affluent homes on the hill, and the mixture of white Georgian semis and new brick terraces that made up Champion Grove, between Denmark Hill Station on one side and East Dulwich Station, at the foot of the hill on the other. The address was at the top of what is now known as Dog Kennel Hill, between the railway to Charing Cross and the railway to London Bridge Station.

The smoke and the occasional shaking from the commuter trains must have been felt in the house. But the green fields also ran from the other side of the street down towards Dulwich and the Crystal Palace, which glinted on the skyline. Camille Pissarro's painting of Lordship Lane Station, a quarter of a century before, showed the view from Dog Kennel Hill and Champion Grove and into the distance. On the other side of the hill, you could look across the smog of late Victorian London. The end of John Ruskin's garden was only 100 yards away, but he had moved out two decades before, complaining about the noise of the trains.

Why Champion Grove? Camberwell was at least London, where Helen was studying, and a financial centre, just at the end of the train line to London Bridge, but it was hardly convenient for Canning Town or Custom House. Denmark

Hill was also, as the name suggests, high enough to avoid the smog – the next hill southwards, from where the huge glinting bulk of the Crystal Palace loomed over the surroundings, was known as the 'fresh air suburb'. There are hints to suggest that he may have been having difficulty with his breathing, as so many people did in smoggy, foggy London in those days.

There may have been another reason he moved here. Camberwell in the 1890s was becoming something of an artist's colony. At least one neighbour was a journalist, and the arrival of the prototype of the South London Fine Art Gallery in 1887 at 207 Camberwell Road, soon to be the Camberwell School of Arts and Crafts, brought London's *avant garde* flocking. The gallery was a project of the Working Men's College, and it was possible that he trained there, but the Camberwell lecture hall was not opened until 1893 and he had been in the area at least three years before that.

Even if Richard was not somehow in Camberwell for the arts, he was living next door to an umbrella manufacturer called Frederick Hart at 4 Champion Grove, I wondered if this might have been a clue, because I found quite by chance that a cousin of his by marriage (Lavinia Boyle) had died in the Camberwell asylum in 1901, presumably from dementia. She was married to Patterson Boyle, living in Oxford Street, also listing himself as an umbrella manufacturer. Their son James also lived in Camberwell (in Mann Street, obliterated in the Blitz). I came to the conclusion this may have been the original reason for moving to Champion Grove: James Boyle had heard about the house for sale through Hart and through his parents.

But somehow this isn't quite the end of the explanation, because Champion Grove was at that time a peculiar, edgy cul-de-sac, almost Bohemian but not quite, almost countryside but not quite. Opposite Richard, at 7 Champion Grove, lived a giant of the Victorian Theatre, Frank Desprez – a successful librettist and friend of D'Oyly Carte's. As the census clerks arrived in the street in 1891, Desprez's most successful work was *The Nautch Girl* or *The Rajah of Chutneypore*, which was then beginning a long run at the Savoy Theatre. For most of his period as Richard's neighbour, he was editor of the London theatre paper *The Era*.

All this raises more questions than it answers. When did Richard Boyle first consider himself an artist, or was that just an immediate way of earning money in 1891? Did he have any formal training? Was it the Arts and Crafts, or even the Anglo-Catholic, aspects of stained glass that excited him, or was he – more likely in the 1890s – a follower of what is now known as the Aesthetic Movement, with their ideology of 'art for art's sake'? He had spent the first half of his life as a staunch Anglican, but was he tiptoeing towards Anglo-Catholicism? I still don't know the answers to these questions but a visit to what was originally called the Camberwell School of Arts did provide some clues.

*

Richard Boyle arrived in Camberwell before the college was opened in 1898, but during the great revolution in adult education that followed the Technical Education Act of 1889, which allowed local authorities to charge a penny on the rates and to use it for training purposes. The South London Technical Art School started in Kennington in 1879 and Goldsmith's College in 1891. In fact, it was when Camberwell's Vestry (the council) took over the art school and moved it to Peckham Road that the basis for launching an art school in Camberwell was in place. The money was given as a memorial to the artist Lord Leighton.

I spent a fascinating morning going through the school's first minutes book, and learning – along with the difficulties of keeping naked models warm and the dim incandescent gas lights they used while they waited for electricity – I found the daily comings and goings of a powerful new institution. The arts and crafts pioneer W. R. Lethaby was at the meetings, the lettering pioneer Edward Johnston was lecturing. It was an exciting time, and especially as the central purpose was to intervene in the local trades and provide th training they needed. They had trouble with the plastering course, for example, until they found a trained plasterer to teach it, and then had to constantly subdivide the course to keep the numbers manageable. The house-painting course was also popular. But it wasn't until 1904 that the school decided to launch a stained glass course. It ran every Tuesday and Thursday at 7.30pm (later every Monday and Thursday).

A little more research provided me with the information about why the course had been launched. Because Camberwell was then a centre of the burgeoning stained glass industry. This seems to me to be the best hypothesis. Richard came to Denmark Hill because he was involved with stained glass, initially as an investor and later as an artist himself.

*

But the most important information in the 1891 census in Champion Grove is what is hidden.

Richard has been at pains to cover his tracks. He was also being careful; he could hardly know, any more than we can, if he was still liable for arrest. He kept his name, but he took the precaution of changing his age and other details. He claimed to have been born in Scotland in 1843, making him six years younger than his actual age. He could afford one servant (Elizabeth Harris), but was obviously being careful with money. In other documents at the time, he was careful to change his middle name from the distinctive 'Warneford' to the much less obvious 'William'.

But the most unexpected element was that there was information about his friend. I only realised this was significant when I saw that Richard's death in 1900 had been registered by someone called Thomas W. Durman (born: Scotland, 1863). I did idly wonder whether the visitor on census day in 1891, called T. W. Penrose Durham (born: Scotland, 1863), sounded much the same. The two names were so similar and they could easily have been misheard by the census collector. It didn't take much to discover that they were one and the same.

The man calling himself 'Penrose Durham' is such an important figure in what follows that it is worth taking a moment to fill in some of his background. He was born in Leith outside Edinburgh on 17 June 1863, the son of Joseph and Mary Durman, and baptised Thomas William.

These were the years of the great agricultural depression when a quarter of the English population left the land and went to the cities over three decades, often to an uncertain industrial future in the new slums and tenements. That is also the story of the Durman family. They came from Chilgrove outside Chichester in Sussex, where Thomas William's grandfather was a gentleman farmer. His son Joseph became a farrier in the Third Light Dragoons, a cavalry regiment with which he presumably took part in the capture of Kabul in 1842 and in the Sikh Wars that followed. Joseph met his wife when he was stationed back in Hampton Court. Mary was illiterate.

By the 1881 census, the Durman family was living in Clapham (6 Pearman Street). Joseph had become a bricklayer and had since died, and Mary was bringing up her family of seven by taking in washing. Thomas William, then eighteen, was calling himself by his second name and was in service. He was working as a footman at Morden Hall next to Morden Park in Surrey, where the head of the household was the banker John Wormald, a director of the private bank Child & Co., now part of the Royal Bank of Scotland group.

Morden Hall had a long connection with finance. The financier Abraham Goldsmith lost a great deal of money in the 1809 stock market crisis, and shot himself in the grounds. I have no direct evidence that Wormald knew Richard Boyle, or that they continued to have any communication with each other after 1884, but Wormald was certainly a frequent visitor to Dublin.

That may explain the peculiar incident in June 1881 when someone called William Durman was arrested and fined for assault on railway staff at Kilmessan Station near Meath outside Dublin. He appeared to be staying at Castle Odder, presumably as part of John Wormald's entourage of servants.

I was able to find out a number of vital details about Thomas William Durman's life after the 1891 census, when he was living with Richard in Champion Grove – but nothing definite for the decade before. Nor where they met – nor what drew two people of such different backgrounds together, a disgraced banker on the way down and a former valet on the way up. So I was never able to discover quite what transformed William Durman, footman, into Penrose Durman, a Roman Catholic convert and clerk to an inventor in an office above a coffee shop in Camomile Street, opposite Liverpool Street Station. A decade is rather a long time to lose track of someone and it also meant that I have never really understood the significance of the name Penrose.

My best explanation is that, if Durman was what the Boyle family believed 'happened again', then Durman simply adopted his camp nickname, rather as Malcolm Johnston had with the name 'Clyde'. Perhaps he had lived for a time in Penrose Street, either in Dublin or – more likely – in Peckham.

It would be tempting to tie Thomas William Penrose Durman into Dublin. He was, after all, exactly the same age as Johnston. Perhaps they even resembled each other. First Johnston and then Durman; it was a progression and, by converting to Catholicism, Durman reveals himself to be at least a fellow traveller in the Aesthetic movement, with its fascination with somewhat camp, Bearsley-esque religion. But the truth is that I don't know.

In particular, it is extremely difficult now, more than a century later, to work out why he needed to disguise his identity in the census. Perhaps, like the notorious male prostitute Dublin Jack, he had a bit part in the Cleveland Street Scandal of 1889, which had come close to involving the heir apparent to the throne, the ill-fated Prince Albert Victor. Perhaps, like so many other former servants, he had lost his position and drifted into the gay substrata and run into trouble under the new laws.

But the only member of the Durman family who was definitely in trouble was Thomas William's younger brother Arthur, who was a barman at the Clarence Tavern, a huge pub at 24 Charing Cross. In November 1892, Arthur Durman was tried for burglary and sentenced to twelve months hard labour. In 1901, he was living in Stangate Street in Lambeth, married and still doing bar work.

My best guess is that Richard hoped he could carry on working as a banker when he arrived in London again from

Germany, some time in the late 1880s, or at least to use his skills as an investor and his financial contacts in London, which must have included John Wormald at Morden Hall. Perhaps that is how he met the man then calling himself William Durman. Perhaps he was hoping to invest in some of the inventions of Durman's later employer Frederick John King. Either way, they met – and their exact relationship may have been known enough to upset Alice Boyle, but was more likely to have been as unknowable to the Boyle family as it is to us. Perhaps the reason Richard chose Denmark Hill to buy a house was simply because it *was* so inaccessible to the family.

All this raises another intriguing possibility. It is impossible to know what kind of relationship these two had together, whether it was friendship – across the class and generation divide – or whether it was more than that. We can say that it certainly seems to have lasted. Most of the most virulent Victorian sex scandals, from Charles Dilke to Oscar Wilde, reserved the real horror for mixing up the classes in sex, and there is an element of this implied here.

We can imagine the attitude of his wider family. Here was their father or their brother, or their estranged husband, living in a strange south London suburb, peddling his skills as an artist, a fully paid up member of the Aesthetic Movement (patrons: O. Wilde and A. Beardsley), and apparently in an ambiguous relationship with another man, a former servant and a Roman Catholic convert. Was he in fact balancing along the very boundaries of the criminal law? Oscar Wilde's own children so felt the force of their father's shame that they changed their names. No wonder Richard was absent from his son's wedding photographs.

Then, some time around 1895, something happened to upset this new life. He disappears from the records in Champion Grove and we can only guess what was going on.

6

"The little bedroom papered red.
The gas's faint malodorous light.
And one beside me in the bed.
Who chatters, chatters, half the night."
Arthur Symons, 'The Dark Angel', 1895

Something was happening to Victorian England in those years after the Dublin Scandal and Labouchère criminalised homosexual behaviour, and it was related to the tension between those twin drives – part of the spirit of the age. One direction was towards the demand for purity of behaviour and the idea that the state could and should legislate for aspects of our sex lives; the other direction was towards a kind of authentic self-assertion. The parallel campaigns against child sex abuse in prostitution and the campaign against gay sex was an uneasy combination. The two issues seem so different to us, but for those late Victorians – disturbed by the rapid social and technological change, from motor cars to telephones and cinemas – the two ideas seemed closely related. Both seemed be driven partly by a projection of people's own loss of innocence – and a fear that young people would be led astray, perverted and ruined.

The events in Dublin in 1884 cast a long shadow, especially because behind some of these fears lay the terrifying power of the mob, revealed in those bonfires and torchlight processions that had shaken Ireland during the Dublin trials. The result had been the peculiarly English phenomenon of the sex scandal.

First, there was Sir Charles Dilke, the radical Liberal MP for Chelsea and the Three-in-a-Bed Scandal, which particularly shocked society because one of the three in Dilke's bed was supposed to have been a servant. Prime minister Gladstone used Labouchère as an intermediary with the wronged husband. Then, in 1890, came the revelation of Charles Stewart Parnell's long-standing affair with Katherine, the wife of his fellow MP William O'Shea, which led to his fall from grace and eventual death – and incidentally destroyed all hope of home rule for Ireland. But it had been the whiff of sexual involvement across the class divide which really shocked people. In fact, in the emerging gay culture there was a fascination for precisely this kind of relationship. Some of it emerges in embarrassing stuff like Edward Carpenter's demand for "the thick-thighed, hot, coarse-fleshed young bricklayer with a strap round his waist", and E. M. Forster's simple request to "love a strong young man of the lower classes and to be loved by him". But for Carpenter, living with the former labourer George Merrill, this was a serious, revolutionary business. Carpenter and the yellow press agreed on this at least: if the two classes slept with each other, Victorian society really would shake.

Then came Cleveland Street, the first gay sex scandal in London, this time involving Prince Albert Victor himself, the eldest son of the Prince of Wales, the royal who gets a walk-on part in the Jack the Ripper conspiracy theories. Once again, the key player came from Dublin.

John Saul, also known as 'Dublin Jack', was said to have been one of the witnesses at the 1884 – though it has never been clear which one and 'John Saul' was clearly not his real name. He had been interviewed in London by Meiklejohn, as Johnston was, but his real claim to fame was as the author of the pornographic autobiography *Sins of the Cities of the Plain*, privately printed in 1881 when Johnston was seventeen, so this probably wasn't him.

Dublin Jack found himself suddenly prominent, appearing for the defence in a libel action brought by the main focus of the story, the man carrying the can for everyone who had frequented the gay brothel at 19 Cleveland Street – Lord Euston. Euston won his case, despite the testimony of John Saul, who detailed the incriminating acts which he had indulged in with Euston as a prostitute, even though he was incriminating himself and could face prosecution too (Lord Arthur Somerset skipped the country).

The man who did most to reveal Cleveland Street to the world, Labouchère again, was furious that Dublin Jack was never prosecuted. But once again, the authorities had stumbled upon the real problem they faced with prominent gay scandals: if there was one thing they feared more than punishing the guilty, it was the revelation of the physical details of what they did in open court.

What made this possible in the first place is that the British public were projecting their own threatened innocence onto their children. Innocence was prized: and the great age of children's writing was now under way. But adults were feeling the loss of their own innocence: by the 1890s, the British had discovered sex, and shocked themselves by finding they enjoyed the conversation. They had known in private, of course, but this was public. It was even the subject for published poetry, for goodness sake – and one could only guess what those Aesthetes got up to. The introduction of contraceptives in 1871 had led to a small revolution in the size of families, dropping from an average of seven or eight over thirty years to just two or three. But it had also led, in the fateful years of 1895, to poet Arthur Symons' slim volume dedicated to his sexual encounters in the night. It was heterosexual this time, and rather naive in its assumptions that both sides were equally charmed by the meetings, but it was available.

Yes, the decadent age seemed to be upon them, and there were those who looked around and knew instinctively who to blame.

*

The arrest and imprisonment of Oscar Wilde was a watershed, but it was predictable given the changing spirit of the age and the monumental clash of these cultures. The previous summer, the police had raided 14 Fitzroy Street and arrested eighteen men, including two wearing women's clothing. It was the changing spirit of the times, as the authorities began to apply the Criminal Law Amendment Act as Labouchère had originally intended.

Wilde's friend, the young artist and writer Max Beerbohm, had even joked about it a few months before. He told to a friend that Wilde and his friend Bosie, Lord Alfred Douglas, had been arrested "for all kinds of crimes" at the Café Royale. It was horribly prescient.

It was the relationship between Wilde and Douglas that was the immediate cause of their difficulties, because it enraged Bosie's father, the pugilist and sportsman the Marquess of Queensberry. From the end of 1893, Queensberry had been subjecting Wilde to a furious series of public scenes, threatening him to stop him seeing his son. Once again, the explicit agenda was not so much the punishment of homosexual behaviour; it was to prevent the perversion of youth. Perhaps even Queensberry was suffering from a sense of lost innocence.

In the spring of 1894, Queensberry sent a peculiarly threatening telegram explaining that he would cut off his son's money if the relationship continued. Bosie replied with his own insulting telegram: "What a funny little man you are."

It was irritating, but it remained a source of humour. When Queensberry threatened to disrupt the opening night of *The Importance of Being Earnest* at the St James's Theatre,

Wilde had him excluded by security guards. He stomped around angrily outside and finally left behind a bunch of vegetables. He may have been aware that 'Earnest' was 1890s slang for gay; he would not have been aware that the main character was called Jack, a reference – or so it is said – to Dublin Jack, whose illicit book Wilde had very much enjoyed.

Finally, it stopped being amusing when Queensberry left a card for Wilde at the Albemarle Club, describing him as "posing as a somdomite" – in his rage, he spelled the word wrong. Stupidly, Wilde was encouraged to sue, remembering perhaps how Gustavus Cornwall had escaped prosecution in Dublin ten years before, though presumably not remembering that he had lost the original libel action.

Wilde was at the height of his fame that spring. The West End in London was alive with his name, his jokes, his famous remarks. Those who wandered by *The Ideal Husband* at the Haymarket Theatre might not have gone in – they might instead have been destined to hear Albert Chevalier or Marie Lloyd at the London Pavilion or the Holborn Empire – but they would have known his name. And because of his prominence, and his symbolic importance as the leader of the Aesthetes and his unconventional opinions on taste and morality, he was about to become a *cause célèbre*, the focus of all the rage that the mob could generate.

The libel trial began on 3 April, with the future creator of Northern Ireland Sir Edward Carson defending Queensberry, and beginning with a series of letter from Oscar to Bosie which had fallen into the hands of the defence. They were signed in rather affected ways: "Always, with undying love, Oscar".

Was this an unusual way for one man to sign a letter to another, asked Carson? Wilde's barrister Sir Edward Clarke challenged Carson to find anything "in the remotest degree, [to] suggest anything hostile in the moral character of Mr Wilde".

Carson went on with a cold-blooded but brilliant cross-examination of Wilde, asking him about his relationship with Alfred Taylor, who appeared to procure young men for older men. Taylor was the wealthy son of a cocoa manufacturer living at 3 Little College Street in Westminster, where he was supposed to have kept women's clothing. He went on to ask Wilde about some of his more outrageous aphorisms: "Wickedness is a myth invented by good people to account for the curious attractiveness of others". Wilde kept the public gallery in stitches with his witty repartee.

The high point of the libel action was the moment that Wilde was asked by Carson about the "love that dare not speak its name". Wilde replied with a flight of impassioned rhetoric that drew applause from the gallery. It is a David-and-Jonathan love between an elder and a younger man, he said. "It is beautiful. It is fine. It is the noblest form of affection. There is nothing unnatural about it."

But when he was asked about his friendships with former valets, dangerous ground as we have seen, he made his fatal slip. Walter Grainger had worked as a servant in Oxford, and waited on him and Douglas when he was sixteen. Had he kissed him, Carson asked?

"Oh dear, no!" said Wilde, playing to the gallery. "He was a peculiarly plain boy. He was unfortunately extremely ugly. I pitied him for it!"

The following day, the jury found for Queensberry and Wilde slipped out by the side door. Queensberry's lawyer sent a note to the Director of Public Prosecutions to inform him that Wilde was now vulnerable to prosecution himself, under the notorious Section 11 of the Criminal Law Amendment Act. Queensberry also sent his own message to Wilde: "If the country allows you to leave, all the better for the country; but, if you take my son with you, I will follow you wherever you go and shoot you."

At 3.30pm on 5 April, Scotland Yard applied to Bow Street magistrates for a warrant for his arrest. It seems likely that the magistrate did the gentlemanly thing and fixed the time for fifteen minutes after the boat train left London for the coast. But Wilde failed to escape. Paralysed by indecision, he had stayed with his closest friends. He was arrested by two policemen at 6.30 that evening at the Cadogan Hotel, sipping hock and seltzer. By the same evening, his name had been removed from the playbills at St James's Theatre.

*

Two trials followed. Wilde found himself accused alongside Alfred Taylor and, at first, the jury failed to agree. Home

Secretary H. H. Asquith decided immediately on a retrial and, this time, they tried Taylor first. By then the writing was on the wall.

Wilde was found guilty on 25 May, the day after Queen Victoria's birthday and the crowds outside were already tinged with patriotic fervour. The judge also passed sentence with a short speech guaranteed to inflame:

"Oscar Wilde and Alfred Taylor, it has never been my lot to try a case of this kind before which has been so bad. One has to put a stern restraint on oneself to prevent oneself describing in language I ought not to use the sentiments which must arise in the breast of every man who has a spark of decent feeling in him..."

He called Wilde "the centre of a circle of extensive corruption among young men of the most hideous kind." As far as he was concerned, the severest sentence – now two years hard labour – was "utterly inadequate".

Wilde made his final attempt to remonstrate, shouting "May I not speak, my lord?" But the shouts of "shame, shame" drowned out his words. Most commentators agreed that, because he was unused to physical labour, the sentence would kill him. The Irish poet Yeats, in London at the time, reported the prostitutes dancing in the street. But it was a fury that required explanation: "The rage against Wilde was also complicated by the Britisher's jealousy of art and the artist," he said later.

Worse in some ways, for Wilde, the audiences for his plays – and therefore his income – rapidly dwindled. His family fled and changed their names. His home in Tite Street, in Chelsea, was repossessed at breakneck speed and his pictures, belongings and clothes were sold by an auctioneer on site at knockdown prices, while people pilfered his manuscripts and notebooks.

"His arrest was the signal for an orgy of philistine rancour such as even London had never known before," wrote the journalist Frank Harris later. "The puritan middle classes, which had always regarded Wilde with dislike as an artist and an intellectual scoffer, a mere parasite for the aristocracy, now gave free scope to their disgust and contempt, and everyone tried to outdo his neighbour in expressions of loathing and abhorrence."

*

There was some link made with the Dublin Scandal which seemed to the newspapers to have started the rot. Wilde seemed to have taken heart from the escape of Gustavus Cornwall in similar circumstances, but the law had changed since then, and he found himself tarred with the Dublin brush. The *Daily Telegraph* claimed that Wilde had "transferred from Trinity College, Dublin to Oxford his vices, his follies and his vanities".

Harris was between editorships and he tried to get an article accepted, anywhere, urging a moderate sentence. But none of his fellow editors would take it. Some weeks later, he heard on the rumour mill that the Prison Commission would accept a letter from the literary world asking for some consideration for Wilde in gaol, reading material or a light in his cell at night. He swung into action and was horrified when two of the leading writers of the age, both friends of Wilde, George Meredith and George Bernard Shaw, refused to sign.

Labouchère crowed in *Truth,* though Wilde had always admired his writing. But Stead wrote a thoughtful editorial in the *Pall Mall Gazette* a few weeks later, afraid that it would mean that the assumed innocence of same sex relationships would be compromised, rather as opposite sex relationships had been. He also returned to his usual theme of class and gender. If Wilde had ruined the lives of young girls, instead of young men, then nobody would have commented, he said – again, this was a panic about the damage done to young people, rather than an explicit campaign against homosexuals in general. Such a concept still barely existed.

He also returned to his favourite theme: the imbalance between the classes – especially given what was known to take place in the nation's exclusive boarding schools. "If all persons guilty of Wilde's offense were to be clapped in gaol, there would be a surprising exodus from Eton, Harrow, Rugby and Winchester, to Pentonville and Holloway."

Lord Alfred Douglas was abroad at this stage – like so many others – but, when he saw Stead's editorial he wrote a surprisingly humane, not to say modern, reply comparing Wilde with his father:

"Oscar Wilde seduced no-one, he did no one any harm. He was a kind, generous and astonishingly gifted man, utterly incapable of meanness or cruelty. Lord Queensberry was divorced from my mother after, for twelve years, she had silently endured the most horrible suffering at his hands."

He wrote a similar reply to Labouchère. Neither editor dared publish, but a copy survived to be used against Douglas in his libel action with the future novelist Arthur Ransome, eighteen years later.

*

Wilde was forced to serve every hour of his two-year sentence. When he was released, on 19 May 1897, the man who dared meet him at the prison gates was the Christian Socialist the Rev Stewart Headlam, who he barely knew, who had also stood bail for him after his arrest. Headlam, also the man who rediscovered William Blake's lost 'Jerusalem' lyric, met him at the gates of Pentonville in a brougham and took him to his home in Bloomsbury. "He was given the first cup of coffee after two years," said his host. "How grateful he was."

I realised that these unnerving events would have been lived through, by Richard Boyle and Penrose Durman, without knowing the outcome that we are so familiar with. For anyone with an outstanding arrest warrant for related accusations, it must have been a frightening period.

I tried to think my way into the mind of my great-great-grandfather. I visited Champion Grove, only to find that the house he owned had been bombed in the Blitz. I peered out across the view that he must have seen from the top of the hill, down towards what was then Champion Hill Station (now East Dulwich). I trudged the familiar pavements on the hills above Camberwell, seeking some kind of connection. I realised that the distinctive shape of the twin tunnels from Denmark Hill platform must have been familiar to them, and the white painted bow windows and front door fanlights too, but it wasn't much.

It was when I made my way to the Metropolitan Archives to look at the street directories and electoral rolls that I got my next surprise. There he was, 'Richard William Boyle' at the address consistently every year through the early 1890s. But at some point in 1895, Richard and Penrose disappear from the record. The house at 8 Champion Grove was let and there was no sign of either of them in any of the directories. I wondered what could possibly have led my great-great-grandfather to flee for a second time.

7

"When first I was put into prison some people advised me to try and forget who I was. It was ruinous advice. It is only by realising what I am that I have found comfort of any kind. Now I am advised by others to try on my release to forget that I have ever been in a prison at all. I know that would be equally fatal. It would mean that I would always be haunted by an intolerable sense of disgrace, and that those things that are meant for me as much as for anybody else – the beauty of the sun and moon, the pageant of the seasons, the music of daybreak and the silence of great nights, the rain falling through the leaves, or the dew creeping over the grass and making it silver – would all be tainted for me, and lose their healing power, and their power of communicating joy."
Oscar Wilde, *De Profundis*

It was this peculiar and unexplained disappearance that set me thinking about the implications of Wilde's arrest at the time, and what it must have seemed like to those who lived through the period. We know now what happened, that Wilde was sent to Holloway and then, famously, to Reading Gaol. We know that the threat to the gay subculture of London was not going to be acted upon. We know now, of course, that the outpouring of public rage would not be turned further against those suspected of the same 'practices' as Wilde, as they put it at the time, at least not systematically. But the newspapers must have been terrifying if you were teetering on the edge of the law, and – at the time – they could not have known what was about to happen.

Both Richard and Penrose, as he was then, were living under inaccurate names. They were also living together, afraid of making this too apparent even to Elizabeth their servant. One of them, and possibly both of them, also had a history. It must have been a fearful moment. Would there have been torchlight processions and burning effigies as there had been in Dublin? Would the baying mob be allowed to rampage? Would the police start tracking down the middle class miscreants, since that was what the people seemed to be demanding? It is hardly surprising that they were nervous.

Nor were they the only ones. Henry Harland, the editor of *The Yellow Book;* reported the packed ferry from Dover the night of Wilde's arrest. Lord Alfred Douglas escaped on the eve of the first trial. "He seemed to have lost his nerve," said Max Beerbohm, and Bosie's reputation clearly followed him across the Channel. The local paper in Le Havre objected to him hiring to young men to crew his yacht, implied that he was corrupting morals in the town, and forced him to escape a second time, this time to Naples. He told French press later that he knew forty or fifty of the best men in society who were homosexual, plus – he added for good measure – hundreds of Oxford undergraduates.

Beardsley was also in Le Havre, having also skipped the country. He was anticipating his dismissal as art editor of *the Yellow Book* by composing a pornographic poem called 'Under the Hill' for a new quarterly called *The Savoy*.

As always, it was left to Frank Harris to say what nobody else put on paper:

"Never was Paris so crowded with members of the English governing classes; here was to be seen a famous ex-minister; there the fine face of a president of a royal society; at one table at the Café de la Paix, a millionaire recently enobled and celebrated for his exquisite taste in art; opposite to him a famous general.... scattered over the continent from Naples to Monte Carlo from Palermo to Seville under all sorts of pretexts."

There was the measure of that moment of fear that gripped England in the late spring of 1895, and it was ironic. For centuries, London had provided a haven from continental tyranny – the Huguenots, the aristocracy fleeing the guillotine, the refugees from the Franco-Prussion War. In only three years' time, the city would offer a temporary home to the great French novelist Emile Zola for his role in the Dreyfus affair ("Never any salt in anything. All the vegetables boiled and served without butter or oil," he complained. "And the bread – good God, English bread, barely cooked, all soft, like a sponge."). But now it was the other way around. Those who were wealthy or desperate enough fled to France, rather than be caught up in the great settling of scores against Wilde and his artistic elite.

Robbie Ross, Wilde's friend who had stuck by him, fled to the Terminus Hotel in Calais and then to Rouen. The gay Scottish politician and sculptor Lord Ronald Gower and Wilde's other defence witnesses at the trial also felt it best to leave. Another one to go, this time to Germany, was the young poet John Gray, a friend of Beardsley's who had been given the money to hire a lawyer with a watching brief during the trials, in case his name was mentioned.

Gray waited until the result of the trail was certain before he left. His reaction at the news of Wilde's arrest was unusual. He headed for the nearest Roman Catholic church, and fell on his knees in front of the statue of the Virgin Mary. The next thing he knew, the cleaning lady was tapping him on the shoulder and saying she was about to lock up. He had been there all day. It was somehow a very 1890s experience, with the weight of sin weighing down on him, just as it seemed to weigh down on society.

Some of the threat that was apparent at the time is obvious from Beerbohm's description of his visit to Scotland Yard at the height of the second trial. He wanted to meet the police inspector responsible for the case and see if it might be possible to intervene for a lighter sentence. Up on the wall above the inspector's desk, Beerbohm was surprised to see his own famous caricature of Oscar Wilde with bulbous lips, a feminine caricature making him resemble a grand dame, the very picture of corrupt camp. "I hadn't realised until that moment how wicked it was," wrote Beerbohm later. "It felt as if I had contributed to the dossier against Oscar."

Looking back to that moment of fear, it becomes clear that other – more frightening – rumours were abroad at the time. One of the reasons that Queensberry was quite so determined to end his son's relationship with Wilde was that he was desperate about the death of his elder son, Lord Francis Douglas, Viscount Drumlanrig. Drumlanrig had been killed in a mysterious shooting accident the previous year, which looked worryingly like suicide. The rumours suggested that he had been in some kind of relationship with Lord Rosebery, the prime minister himself.

Rosebery himself appeared to be in the grip of some kind of breakdown during these months. He was suffering from such serious insomnia that he was feeling suicidal. It seems possible that he was also coming under intense pressure from Queensberry. Certainly, reports suggested that the government had almost ground to a halt before the Wilde trial, terrified of a nameless threat they could hardly articulate, and the Liberal Party was heading for their catastrophic general election defeat that summer.

What this means, perhaps, is that it was not just friends of Oscar Wilde, nor people in the semi-shadows like Richard and Penrose, who could smell the threat that loomed so terrifyingly that April and May. The establishment itself was frightened of the consequences if the prime minister being dragged into one almighty homosexual scandal, that threatened to drag down the whole regime, cabinet, royal family and all.

Recent research suggests that Rosebery had not been involved with anyone from Queensberry's family, but that isn't the point. The prime minister was known, by those in the know, to be heavily sedated and taking long midnight drives by himself. The rumours were enough to scare. This is how one newspaper put it, in a note under the reports of Wilde's arrest, at the moment of great fear, on 6 April 1895 (the *Hartlepool Mail*, based on Press Association reports):

"A correspondent writes: I hear to-night in the lobby on excellent authority that the Oscar Wilde case is likely to have a most sensational sequel. If the rumours which are afloat to-night should prove to be correct, we shall have such an exposure as has been unheard of for many years past. Many shrewd guesses have been made as to the identity of the mysterious 'Mr B'."

What would the rest of the public have made of that? Would 'such an exposure' imply to them a particular person, or would it imply widespread arrests? Would it have reassured anyone on the fringes of the affair who happened also to have a surname beginning with 'B'? I am suggesting that this was a unique moment of panic for those driven underground by Section 11, and that it seemed only sensible for people to take the opportunity for a continental visit.

My impression is that Richard Boyle had few enough resources, except for his home in Champion Grove. But he went, and Penrose Durman went with him. None knows where, as Max Beerbohm would have said.

*

Those who fled filtered home again when the fuss had died down, and it was clear that the Wilde case had not been the start of some kind of sexual purge. Richard Boyle was among them. By 1897, he was renting cheap lodgings in an anonymous section of inner city Lambeth (74 Stamford Street), more in the Durman family's territory than his own.

Durman certainly must have been home by the previous year, because in 1896 he took over a pub, presumably an investment by friends. The document of exchange still exists for the Surrey Drovers pub in the Selsden Road, demolished in 1935. It lists his full name, Thomas William Penrose Durman.

It is hard to know quite what to read into this, whether this was Richard Boyle's way of supporting him in a profession or whether it represented, instead, a burst of independence. Whatever it was, the arrangement did not last, and three years later – by 1899 – he was the landlord of the Rising Sun pub at 24 Blackfriars Road (later the Paper Moon), near Blackfriars Bridge. Since this is a few minutes walk from their address in Stamford Street it seems likely that the rented accommodation was chosen because it was convenient for the pub.

But Richard's lungs were suffering and he clearly missed the fresh air, and the strange hint of bohemianism in Champion Grove. By the end of the decade, he was back, renting the house next door to the one he owned, 6 Champion Grove. He was by then short of breath and suffering from heart trouble. Camberwell's smoke and smog can't have helped, but it was probably a relief compared with Canning Town, and certainly with Lambeth. He may also have been short of money.

As Christmas 1900 approached, the weather took a turn for the worse. There were serious storms across Ireland and the West, the White Star liner *Majestic* had to divert into Liverpool, and the rain battered the English towns and villages – except in London. There, the day before Christmas Eve, a dense fog descended which mixed with the smoke from a million chimneys to create a thick noxious gas. The lines into south east London were especially badly affected, with passengers abandoning trains at London Bridge. Denmark Hill was still not high enough to escape, and even those who lived in airy Champion Hill found themselves struggling for breath. I suspect that Richard had been short of breath for some time, through the warm, balmy summer of 1900, after the excitement of the relief of Mafeking, and now – as the moment approached that marked what people then regarded as the start of the new century – he seems to have become weaker. The papers were full of Kitchener's march north in South Africa and the after-effects of the storm, but the Christmas smog that year seems to have been the final straw.

He died at 6 Champion Grove the day after Boxing Day 1900, just a few days before Queen Victoria – his life exactly matching the 63 years of her reign. With him when he died was the man now calling himself Thomas Durman, a 36-year-old licensed victualler. The cause of death was given as emphysema, heart disease and syncope (fainting). It is tempting to imagine that the upheaval of the second flight fatally undermined his health.

My own family tree gives the year of his death as 1901. Durman registered the death himself, and this time with Richard's distinctive full name and correct date of birth. Both facts imply that his family was not present and may not have even known he was ill. I believe he was in touch with his daughter Helen, by then living in Hove, but have never discovered whether he was ever reconciled with anyone in the rest of his family (his wife Alice died in 1921).

He left just less than £5,000, but had not updated his will since immediately before the scandal. The role of executor therefore fell to his estranged wife, then also living in London, at (91 Belgrave Road in Pimlico). The sum of £5,000 was rather more than the value of his house in Champion Grove, worth about half a million in today's money (rather less than what the Champion Grove house costs now). Either way, through principle or because he simply overlooked it – or because he died unexpectedly – his will pre-dated his relationship with Thomas William Penrose Durman.

The letters have long since disappeared, and we will never know the truth, but I sense discomfort about the will. I have a feeling that all those letters that still existed in the generations that followed had something to do with Richard Boyle and his unplanned, unexplained, untouchable legacy.

Thomas had a difficult life after Richard died, moving from job to job. The Rising Sun did not last. Neither did the tenancy that he took over at 6 Champion Grove.

He stayed living in Champion Grove after Richard's death, but moved to No. 10, where he lodged in one room with another local writer, the historian Francis Badham, who lived there by himself, bashing out articles. Badham was a controversialist, whose only full-length book described how the gospels were written, but at the time he was shocking his contemporaries with a series of attacks on the great English hero, Horatio Nelson. There is something about Champion Grove at the time which still reeked of bohemians.

But Thomas William Penrose was clearly struggling by himself. At one stage, and for one day – Boxing Day 1906 – he was even admitted to the nearby Newington Workhouse, before being sent to hospital. It is from this document that I found out that he had converted to Roman Catholicism, and describing himself – somewhat ominously – as a 'traveller'. He seems also to have been smoking too much.

Not long afterwards, he was describing himself instead as a 'political agent', presumably for the double general elections about the House of Lords in 1910 and 1911. There was something of a jack of all trades, or master of none, about Durman. He doesn't seem to have been successful running a pub or in politics, and once the political crisis was over, he was describing himself as an actor. By then, he had moved again – across the road – to 11 Champion Grove. He died of throat cancer in the Camberwell Infirmary in May 1913. He was only forty-nine.

*

By then, most of those involved in the tumultuous events in Dublin and London had also died. I have been unable to trace what happened to Malcolm Johnston, but the Rev Thomas Dancer Hutchinson – the man who nicknamed him Lady Constance Clyde – ended up living with his unmarried sisters in Ebury Street in London's West End. Martin Kirwan, one of the defendants, died in Galway in 1904. Gustavus Cornwall went with his wife to live on her family estate in Linlithgow and died in 1903.

Ex-inspector John Meiklejohn, the blackmailing detective, died the same month that the *Titanic* sank in 1912. He had eked out his living as a columnist for the *Leeds Mercury.* In 1903, he made the mistake of pursuing a libel action, which was thrown out by the judge on the grounds that he had no reputation that could be damaged.

And on the *Titanic*'s maiden voyage that month was another key player, heading to New York. W. T. Stead did not survive.

As for Labouchère, he had been vetoed for the cabinet by Queen Victoria herself in 1892 and was later accused of insider trading. He criticised fraudulent companies in *Truth* and then, when the value of their shares went down – because readers had followed his advice and dumped them – he bought them himself. He eventually gave up his political career, aware that he would never be promoted to the diplomatic position that suited his talents, as he saw them, and resigned his parliamentary seat to live in Florence. Before he left London, he was finally made a privy councillor and spent the whole ceremony making pointed remarks under his breath. He died in Florence, also in 1912.

Oscar Wilde's death was enlivened by his last witty remark – "this wallpaper is killing me," he is supposed to have said, on his death bed in Paris. "One of us must go."

He died on 30 November 1900, exactly twenty-seven days before Richard Boyle, from meningitis brought on by a wound to the ear, complicated by a fall in prison some years before. He was received into the Catholic Church a few hours before he died. His wife Constance, who had wanted to be reconciled, had died not long before.

Frank Harris dined with him not long before his death, at the Café de la Regence in Nice. An English couple sat down at the next door table, and the man stared. "Do you know who that is," he said, loudly, to his wife. "It's that infamous Oscar Wilde. Fancy his showing himself in public!"

Wilde blanched. "I had already seen that a heavy glass pitcher of water was within reach of my hand," wrote Harris later. "If the man had said one word more, I would have smashed his face with the pitcher."

Instead, he turned to him said: "Your rudeness can be heard; any more if it and you'll be sorry. Now you had better go to another room." Harris was well known there and the manager heard the commotion and asked the couple to leave.

"Good God, Frank," said Wilde. "How dreadful. Why do they hate me so; what harm have I ever done them?"

"Think of London fog," said Harris. "It prevents them from seeing clearly; don't bother about them. Didn't Shakespeare call it 'this all-hating world'."

*

There are few redeeming features about the story of Oscar Wilde. The novelist Compton Mackenzie unveiled a blue plaque to commemorate him on his old violated home in Tite Street. That was in October 1954, and you might think it was a sign that the tide was beginning to change, were it not for the fact that Alan Turing had killed himself after being convicted under Section 11 only seven months before.

As for the story of my great-great-grandfather, I still didn't know as much as I would like – though there was still a revelation to come – but the story seemed a tragic one. I could think of only one silver lining: Richard Boyle's eldest daughter Helen inherited her father's fascination for health, and particularly for public health. She devoted her life to her pioneering women's hospital in Hove, and to the kind of fund-raising her father had helped to manage for hospital causes in Dublin.

Dr Helen Boyle was also fascinated by mental health, particularly about the business of how ordinary people can stay mentally healthy, and the vital importance of providing some kind of respite before people faced a crisis. Towards the end of her life, she was elected as president of the National Council of Mental Hygiene, later MIND, which she had helped found.

At one of their lectures at the Brighton Pavilion, on 8 November 1934, she talked about family life:

"The strong silent man is by no means always an asset in the family. Honesty is the best policy here as elsewhere, honesty and sincerity of soul..."

It is tempting to think that maybe she was thinking there about her father, and the consequences of pretence, but also the consequences of not pretending too. Her only recorded remark about her father was that he had "blotted his copybook". This is undoubtedly true and understates the affair in a forgiving and perhaps even a loving way. It is possible to see her whole career in mental health, not just as a continuation of her father's work in public health, but as a response to the his fall from grace – aware that anyone can call, and we are all prone to the kind of mistaken tactics and misjudgements (if they were misjudgements) which had allowed his fall to happen. She specialised in healing tortured minds. She would have sensed, before most, what was wrong with the advice given by one traditional character in E. M. Forster's hidden novel *Maurice*, about love between men across the class divide: "The worst thing I could do for you is to discuss it".

But then we don't know if Richard's mind was, in fact, tortured. It may be that he found a kind of freedom and fulfilment in Camberwell, and in painting glass, and in his new friendship, that brought him some honesty and peace. But then that is the greatest mystery of all: how did a man who was a leading Dublin banker and Unionist, a justice of the peace, manage to hold together his life when he was a glass artist living in bohemian south London on the fringes of the criminal law? Which was the real Richard Warneford Boyle? What was the relationship between the two?

8

"Nothing's the same for anyone. That's why life's this Hell, if you do a thing you're damned, and if you don't you're damned."
E. M. Forster, *Maurice*

It doesn't seem entirely accurate to describe Richard Boyle as my ancestor. It seems somehow too distant. His daughter was very much part of my upbringing, though she died immediately before I was born in 1958. We spent our summers at her home on the South Downs, and I live near there today myself. My grandfather had a trial for the Ireland national rugby squad in the 1920s because his own grandfather had been born in Ireland. I never quite understood this Irish theme in my background – but I do now.

Chasing down the truth about him was an unexpected and absolutely absorbing task. Months would go by without any kind of breakthrough. On one occasion, I was thrilled to discover some inexplicable letters about him and his wife Alice that were listed in the Berkshire County Archives in Reading. I dashed down and there they were, along with his marriage contract on vellum, in absolutely pristine condition, the paper unfaded, the ink as sharp as it had been the day it had been used. Unfortunately, they were all about life insurance.

Ironically, the final surprise came after a celebration of his daughter Helen, when a blue plaque was unveiled for her in 2015 on the side of what had been the Lady Chichester Hospital. The Serbian ambassador came to make a short speech, because she had been part of the volunteer medical unit that went to Serbia in 1914. I ran into Val Brown, who had written a fascinating book about the hospital and about Helen herself (*Women's Hospitals in Brighton and Hove*), and confided in her about what I had discovered. She asked me where Helen's father had been buried. I said I assumed it was in south London, but that I had never discovered.

The next day she sent me link to a website listing his name among the graves in Camberwell Old Cemetery. There is now a website where you can search for such things, though you have to pay a subscription to find out more exact details. I sat down immediately and subscribed. There was his name, buried there on the very last day of 1900. To my surprise, I found that there was someone buried with him. I clicked on the details: the name was Thomas William Durman.

I stared at the screen trying to take in the implications. They were buried together. I had no idea and, for a moment, I felt quite tearful. It was a moving discovery at the end of so many frustrating glimpses.

Of course, I realised, I must not read too much into it. There are many reasons why they might have been buried together, thirteen years apart. Thomas (as he was now) might not have been able to afford a grave for himself. It may have just been convenient – he was down on his luck, ill and possibly almost penniless when he died, and there was space in the grave. But even so, it was somehow comforting that they did not lie alone. They had lived with each other for at least nine years. Had fled with each other in the middle of that period, invested in pubs with each other, had shared the risks and the rewards, had tiptoed into the Arts and Crafts world around them in Camberwell. It didn't necessarily imply that they loved each other, but it was appropriate somehow that they should have been buried together nonetheless.

*

I could not quite leave it there either. I phoned the office they have set up in Camberwell New Cemetery, part of Southwark Borough Council's ministry of death, and made an appointment. By the time I walked through the footpath, through the graveyard from Honor Oak Station, I felt that I had at least one foot in 1900 myself. I could almost imagine I was looking across the smoky skyline to St Paul's Cathedral, watching the horse-buses wobble by, with their advertising hoardings for Bovril, Lipton's Tea and Rackham's Liver Pills, smell the dung on the streets, dodge the creaking black bicycles. I edited the view and removed anything twentieth century or after. Everything I saw, I saw from the perspective of a century and a decade and a half before. It became a little hypnotic.

I liked the lady behind the desk, who listened to my story and settled down at the computer. Then she heaved an enormous bound volume off the shelf, and opened it up, and showed me the entry. Thomas had bought the grave himself, sometime in 1900, and had paid a little less than £5 for it – or about two months rent. It was difficult to draw many other conclusions from the spidery entry in black ink. I knew the old cemetery was very overgrown in places. I had intended to bring pruning shears but, at the last moment, I had forgotten.

"Can I find it?" I asked.

"You may be able to, but you'll need a map. Wait here a moment."

It was in an overgrown area but I was in luck. It was only in the second row. I would probably not need to climb through creepers and brambles. The map showed the plot numbers and nothing else. It looked impossible, a strange diagram of squares with five-figure numbers all over, but it struck me that I might be able to identify the right place by asking the name of the grave in front. The lady confirmed what I guessed: there was never a headstone.

"Are you driving?"

"No, I said," waving my briefcase. "I'm on foot."

I felt proud of myself for walking, but – since there was a bus passing as soon as I got out of the gates – I caught it anyway. It jerked me back from my Victorian dreamworld.

Camberwell Old Cemetery is not big, but it seems big because so much of it is deeply overgrown. It was also almost empty of the living. I walked through the gates, passed the large modern graves in white marble, and the memorials for beloved children killed in Mesopotamia or Flanders, and made it down one of the avenues to the right. You could dimly discern modern life beyond the graves, the tall flats and the double decker buses going by, but the stillness around me was echoing and eerie. These Victorian graveyards in London are truly cities of the dead, and reading the heart-breaking tributes as I walked past, stretching back generations, was enough to convince me that life is certainly a veil of tears. I was aware also that this is the frame of mind you get into by searching through cemeteries.

The avenue was darker because of the mature trees and undergrowth on either side. I saw that the five-figure plot numbers were written on the front of most of the graves, but they seemed to bear no relation to my map. Was I in the wrong avenue perhaps? I began to despair. I could not face going back to the office to admit defeat.

Then I wondered: was I holding the map upside down? I looked on the other side and, sure enough, there were the numbers I was reading on the map. For some reason I had assumed their grave would be on the left. The next problem were the notices warning of Japanese knotweed and forbidding entry, but the numbers indicated that I had gone beyond them. Then there was the name I had been looking for in front, and I had found the right place.

I stood beside the unmarked grave, though it was not recognisable as such. There were some saplings, and rough grass and scrub that had grown up on top. If we had not been in a Victorian graveyard, it would have looked like the growth you find in an unkempt, uncared for meadow. There was no litter. It just looked as if it was a completely forgotten place. I tried to imagine what it would have been like in the cold and ice, on the last day of 1900, without the trees around us. There was the coffin being lowered in; there was Thomas by the graveside, and Rev Eyre Kidson officiating – perhaps a few friends from Champion Grove. Probably no relatives, though Helen may have been there, tall and thin and shivering. It was, perhaps, the burial of an exile.

Why hadn't I brought some flowers, I asked myself as I walked away? Because I had hardly believed I would find the right spot, and because nobody seemed to be selling flowers in the particular corner on the borders of Peckham, Dulwich and Honor Oak. I walked back again and said a small prayer for my great-great-grandfather. I had searched for him for so long I almost felt I knew him – as much as you know any of your parents and grandparents, perhaps. I asked their forgiveness for revealing those things they had tried so hard to keep hidden, then I said the Lord's Prayer, and Hail Mary for Thomas.

Then I turned back to the world of the living, and left them behind.

*

"I have no doubt we shall win, but the road is long and red with monstrous martyrdoms." That was Oscar Wilde's verdict on the long campaign to make homosexual love acceptable and legal. He was right. But why did it go so wrong so quickly?

This short book suggests that there are serious dangers when political campaigns wrap themselves in populist intolerance in order to drag down an elite. That is what happened in Dublin in 1883/4 and within four decades, the nationalist cause had been won; perhaps not because of the sexual accusations and cruelties. But those had unpredicted and unpredictable effects, not just in Ireland but across the British Isles. Perhaps the real question was why it had those effects, and why this horror of homosexuality swept the nation as swiftly and for as long as it did.

There is a paradox here. In some ways, the final decade and a half of the nineteenth century was very unlike our own time – stuffy, class-ridden, snobbish and divided. In other ways, it was remarkably like our time after all,

The similarities are also down to the unchanging nature of London life. We live at many of the same addresses as they did in the 1890s. We travel by the same numbered bus routes. We watch the same matches: a crowd of 100,000 people watched the FA Cup final in 1900 (Bury 4, Southampton 0). More than today. Everyone involved in these stories are now dead, but we understand them, and could communicate with them if they mysteriously came back to life – and they would understand us.

Like our own time, this was a period of huge social and technological upheaval. We have the internet and mobile phones; they had motor cars and home telephones. We both have a craze for weekend cycling. We both have Sherlock Holmes; we both dream of a detective who can penetrate through the fog and see the truth in the corruption of the inner cities.

We both have huge influxes into our urban areas. We both have agitation about gender relations. We both have outrage about child sexual abuse – emerging in the space of two years in the 1980s, just as it emerged in the 1880s. We both have a sense that the innocence of our children and young people are under threat.

So at the heart of the somewhat accidental criminalisation of homosexual behaviour in 1885, there is another strange apparent contradiction. The great intolerance, and the wave of fear, emerged out of a campaign to protect children from abuse. It was set in motion by deeply tolerant people – Josephine Butler, W. T. Stead, and the Liberal philosopher T. H. Green, who provided the justification for the state to challenge public and private morality. It is no coincidence that the old Gladstonian Liberalism died with the party's defeat in 1895, after Rosebery's struggling government ground to a halt. The 'New Liberalism' was born as a result, and it allowed for state sponsored moral activism.

Even the Dublin Scandal and the three trials of Oscar Wilde are ambiguous, perhaps more so now that they would have seemed a few decades ago. In both cases, a few of the young men involved were probably what we would now describe as 'underage'.

Society in the 1890s was caught in the tension between the drive, not perhaps so much for purity, but for the possibility of innocence – and the drive for some kind of self-determination, self-definition. We are too: they are the two sides of any kind of gender or sexual politics – part demanding to take part, part demanding the right to refuse. These are not contradictory causes, but they tend to attract different kinds of people to the campaign.

So, on the one hand, there was Wilde and his friends pushing forward the boundaries of what could be said and how to love. "I've been married three times in my life," he confessed to French friend, "once to a woman and twice to men." On the other hand, there were campaigners like Stead and his National Vigilance Association pressing for more sexual regulation. Perhaps they could co-exist, as they do in our own time, but then they clashed: in *De Profundis*, Wilde's bitter memoir, he accused Queensberry of all people of trying to be a hero for the purity campaigners. He never could have been, but you can see why anyone might have been confused. Perhaps when you believe that homosexual sex is thrilling because it is forbidden, as Wilde did, then there is bound to be a clash: "Like feasting with panthers," he said.

Perhaps that populist rage and fear is never far below the surface. Either way, when the Irish nationalists tried to drag down the moral position of the protestant ascendancy, they lit the fuse that would also lead to the homosexual laws too. Because, just as the Victorians were afraid that sex across the class divide would bring traditional social distinctions crashing down, the accusations of improper sex could also bring power imbalances crashing down too. It worked both ways. It is a potentially terrifying weapon to use, but it can have unpredictable effects.

*

"If you only had an inkling what the secret was," said one world-weary Duke of Strathmore, probably the Queen Mother's father, "you would go down on your knees and thank God it was not yours." He was telling his long-suffering wife that he had finally been given the family secret by his solicitor, and he did not welcome the news.

Not every family is burdened with the Secret of Glamis, but secrets are double-edged swords in families. If they are distant enough, they are have a thrilling caché, a glamour about them. But too close, and the secrets seem tawdry and embarrassing, even horrific. Their baleful influence stretches down the generations.

Perhaps every family has some of these. Perhaps every individual does. Certainly my own family had protected their late Victorian secret, and the last letters relating to the disgrace of my great-great-grandfather were burned in the 1970s, for fear that somehow they could still hurt and damage the new generation. But then, even without me knowing any of the details, the events had acted on my life, though I was born more than eighty years later. It determined that I should live in London and not Dublin, like my ancestors. It made me English and not Anglo-Irish. It determined what school I should go to. But more than that, I believe, it added just a faint frisson to the older generation, an extra nervousness about our behaviour and peculiarities that hung in the air – as if this nameless secret had seeped into our genes and must be most carefully watched.

This book has tried to name the secret at last; to show some compassion to my ancestor, Richard Warneford Boyle and to bring him in from the cold.

Other titles by David Boyle

Building Futures

Funny Money: In search of alternative cash

The Sum of our Discontent

The Tyranny of Numbers

The Money Changers

Numbers (with Anita Roddick)

Authenticity: Brands, Fakes, Spin and the Lust for Real Life

Blondel's Song

Leaves the World to Darkness

News from Somewhere (*editor*)

Toward the Setting Sun

The New Economics: A Bigger Picture (with Andrew Simms)

Money Matters: Putting the eco into economics

The Wizard

The Little Money Book

Eminent Corporations (with Andrew Simms)

Voyages of Discovery

The Human Element

On the Eighth Day, God Created Allotments

The Age to Come

What if money grew on trees (*editor*)

Unheard, Unseen: Submarine E14 and the Dardanelles

Broke: How to survive the middle class crisis

Alan Turing: Unlocking the Enigma

Peace on Earth: The Christmas truce of 1914

Jerusalem: England's National Anthem

Give and Take (with Sarah Bird)

People Powered Prosperity (with Tony Greenham)
Rupert Brooke: England's Last Patriot
How to be English

Printed in Great Britain
by Amazon